LEGENDS

First published in 2014

A catalogue record for this book is available from the British Library

ISBN: 978-0-85733-728-3

Published by Haynes Publishing, Sparkford, Yeovil,
Somerset BA22 7JJ, UK
Tel: 01963 442030 Fax: 01963 440001
Int. tel: +44 1963 442030 Int. fax: +44 1963 440001
E-mail: sales@haynes.co.uk
Website: www.haynes.co.uk

Haynes North America Inc., 861 Lawrence Drive,
Newbury Park, California 91320, USA

Images © Mirrorpix

Creative Director: Kevin Gardner
Designed for Haynes by BrainWave

Printed and bound in the US

When FOOTBALL Was FOOTBALL

LEGENDS

Adam Powley

Contents

Stan the legendary man.

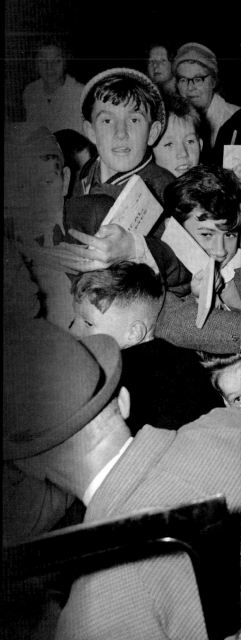

Introduction

What makes a legend? The usual definition applies to an individual renowned in their own time and beyond. When it comes to footballers, it is a label bandied about with increasing frequency. These days, coming on as a sub to score a winning goal in a high-profile Premier League match, or looking good in a Champions League encounter can often confer instant legend status.

But the real legends are those whose qualities last for longer than a brief clip on YouTube. The real legends are the ones whose achievements and qualities stand the test of time – players that people still talk in awe about long after their playing days have ended. Their glory days are recalled in terms of how they rose above their peers to display their singular talents, achievements and character.

It is these qualities that mark out the players featured in this illustrated celebration of great footballers. The players who endeared themselves to club, country or both; the individuals who put their bodies on the line in the name of the cause; the team players who stayed loyal despite temptations to move elsewhere.

It's not simply about the best footballers. Becoming a legend often involves something more than outrageous skill, or an unerring ability to find the back of the net. For that reason this book does not claim to select the greatest players, but more to reflect the varied ways a player can become so popular. Whatever the criteria, any selection will always be subjective. This is just one gallery of greats. While it begins with a prewar legend, it focuses on the postwar era, and the golden decades from the 1950s to the 1970s. As such, it represents the game as it developed through this era, ending just as the Premier League and Champions League arrived to transform the sport.

Many of the individuals featured in the following pages symbolize something beyond their own characteristics. The stories of these players are the stories of the game – from a time when players were honest and dutiful servants, to the lifting of the maximum wage cap and the advent of the pop-star footballer. This is a story about the changing sport as much as it is about the individuals who were its icons.

An editorial choice has been made to focus on British players and their honours in the English League, rather than for example, Scottish trophies. That is not to diminish those achievements, nor to ignore the wonderful foreign players that have graced the game, but simply to provide a portrait of the domestic sport and 40 of its most high-profile, home-grown exponents over a 70-year period.

There is a mixture of players – from the dazzling goalscorers to the more humble but no less vital 'water carriers'. Inevitably most of those featured played for the biggest clubs, but an attempt has been made to represent a range of clubs rather than focus on just a handful.

It's a selection that should have some readers nodding in agreement, but will no doubt enrage others for the absentees who didn't make the cut. That's part of the beauty of the game – we will all have differing views on what makes a legend. The one thing we can be sure of is that while we consider the players of the past there are new ones emerging now who will be forging their own legendary status.

> *"He belongs to the company of the supremely great, like Beethoven, Shakespeare and Rembrandt."*
>
> Bill Shankly

DIXIE DEAN

Everton hero, goalscoring phenomenon, inter-war great, Dixie Dean was the English centre-forward who set the standard all marksmen have tried – and invariably failed – to match.

Winning the FA Cup with Everton in 1933, after a 3-0 win over Manchester City. Dean was one of the scorers.

The clock was ticking down. Five minutes left to make history. And then the moment came. Alec Troup floated a centre into the Arsenal penalty area and the tough but technically accomplished 21-year-old centre-forward yet again got his head to a ball to guide it into the net. It was his third of the match – and his 60th of a quite extraordinary season.

William Dean was his name but fans of not only Everton but of any loyalty around the country and beyond will forever remember him as Dixie. He didn't just rewrite the history books so much as close them. That astonishing total of 60 goals, set in one remarkable, title-winning season for the Toffees, is highly unlikely ever to be matched, let alone surpassed in the English top flight. It was a once-in-lifetime season from a one-off player.

Dean was born into a large family in Birkenhead, the son of a railwayman and a product of one of the most fertile regions in the country for seeding and nurturing football talent. Drawn to the bustling port across the Mersey, he was raised as an Everton fan, but he would have to wait for his opportunity to don the blue shirt. Having left school at 14 to work as a fitter in the railway yards, his exploits with a local club side alerted Tranmere, who signed Dean in 1923.

A prolific 27 League goals in 30 games later (and after losing a testicle in a reserve match), Dean was spotted by Everton scout Tom McIntosh and was soon on his way to immortality thanks to a £3,000 transfer fee. Dean was an immediate success at Goodison, notching 32 goals in his first full season in 1925–26, just six short of the existing League record. That looked easily within Dean's grasp until disaster struck, and he was almost killed in a motorcycle accident. He was lucky to survive, having sustained a fractured skull and a broken jaw. His career certainly seemed to be over. But miraculously, he battled back to full fitness within four months and scored 21 goals in the remaining 27 games of the season, before going on to make his England debut.

Dean appeared to be a phenomenon and – unsurprisingly – myths grew up around the player. A joke did the rounds that a metal plate had been inserted into his skull, and it was this that enabled Dean to score so many goals with his head. Then there was his exotic nickname. One version was that it stemmed from his dark complexion and an association with the American Deep South (or Dixie) another that it was a corruption of an old childhood nickname of "Diggsy". Whatever the truth, it all added to the allure of the most compelling of footballers.

Dean was physically strong, but not overly so. What made him special was his quick thinking and ability to sniff out a chance – the innate skill of all great strikers to be in the right place at the right time. That underpinned his extraordinary achievement in 1927–28.

As Everton marched towards the title, Dean's goals dictated the pace. He scored 14 in the first nine games, including five against Manchester United. By January he had overcome Everton's 38-goal club record tally for a single season. The First Division benchmark of 43 was then breached. As spring arrived, Dean

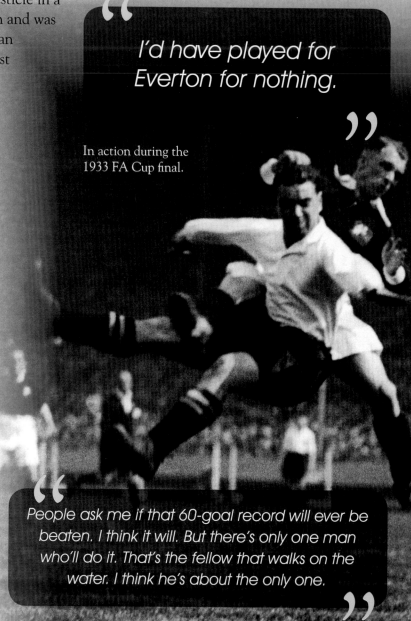

I'd have played for Everton for nothing.

In action during the 1933 FA Cup final.

People ask me if that 60-goal record will ever be beaten. I think it will. But there's only one man who'll do it. That's the fellow that walks on the water. I think he's about the only one.

FOOTBALL
—STATS—

Dixie Dean

Name: William Ralph Dean
Born: Birkenhead, 22nd January 1907
Died: 1st March 1980
Position: Striker
Playing career: 1923–40

Club	Appearances	Goals
Tranmere	33	27
Everton	433	383
Notts County	9	3

Country	Appearances	Goals
England	16	18
TOTAL	**491**	**431**

Honours	
League Title	2 (1927–28, 1931–32)
FA Cup	1 (1933)

was closing in on Middlesbrough's George Camsell, whose overall Football League tally of 59 goals in a season had been set just a year before. The hat-trick against Arsenal sealed the honour. Even a late equalizer for the visitors could not dampen the raucous celebrations.

Such a shining achievement was a near-impossible act to follow but Dean did not disappoint, rattling them in for the next nine years, staying loyal through relegation, and then captaining the side to another League Championship triumph and an FA Cup victory in 1933. That final was the first to feature numbered shirts – with Everton taking numbers 1 to 11 and Manchester City 12 to 22 – and so Dean was, naturally, the first player to wear the coveted number 9 for Everton. Spells at Notts County and then in Ireland with Sligo Rovers preceded his retirement from football and a return to work in civvy street as a publican and in employment with Littlewoods Pools.

England had also been the beneficiaries of Dean's prodigious talent. He scored twice on his international debut against Wales in 1927 and grabbed a brace against Scotland at Hampden Park to end a 23-year run of the Scots' domination of England on Scottish soil. He scored a remarkable 18 goals in just 16 internationals, including hat-tricks against Belgium and Luxembourg.

Dean was the superstar of the age and was the focus of great attention for his astonishing strike rate. But the man himself was very much a team player. He recognized that while his goals made the headlines, they were the product of a collective effort. In 1936, as his Goodison career was winding down, he welcomed as his team-mate Tommy Lawton, the precocious teenager drafted in to play alongside the old master. Dean might have been expected to harbour some resentments, but if he did, he didn't express them. "I know you've come here to take my place," Dean told Lawton. "Anything I can do to help you, I will. I promise, anything at all."

It was a measure of the man. Dean could be hard – a prerequisite for tough times both on and off the pitch – but he was fair. He was never booked, let alone sent off. He was often described as kindly, generous and extrovert, but not arrogant, and certainly not one to boast. He grew up an Everton fan and passed away as one, aged 73 in March 1980 during a derby game against Liverpool at Goodison Park.

RIGHT: Pulling pints and showing off his England caps in the pub Dean ran, the Dublin Packet in Chester, 1950.

TED DRAKE

The great Arsenal side that dominated English football during the 1930s featured many great players, but few were as influential or as popular – and none made such a rapid impact – as Ted Drake.

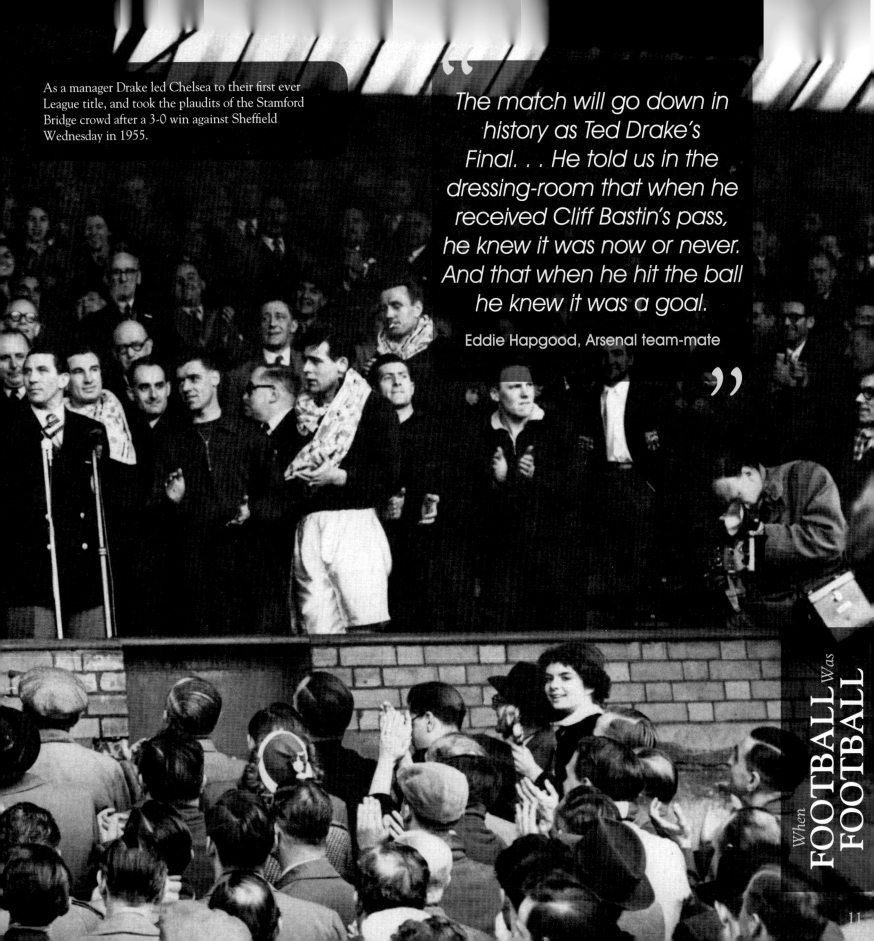

As a manager Drake led Chelsea to their first ever League title, and took the plaudits of the Stamford Bridge crowd after a 3-0 win against Sheffield Wednesday in 1955.

"The match will go down in history as Ted Drake's Final. . . He told us in the dressing-room that when he received Cliff Bastin's pass, he knew it was now or never. And that when he hit the ball he knew it was a goal.

Eddie Hapgood, Arsenal team-mate

"

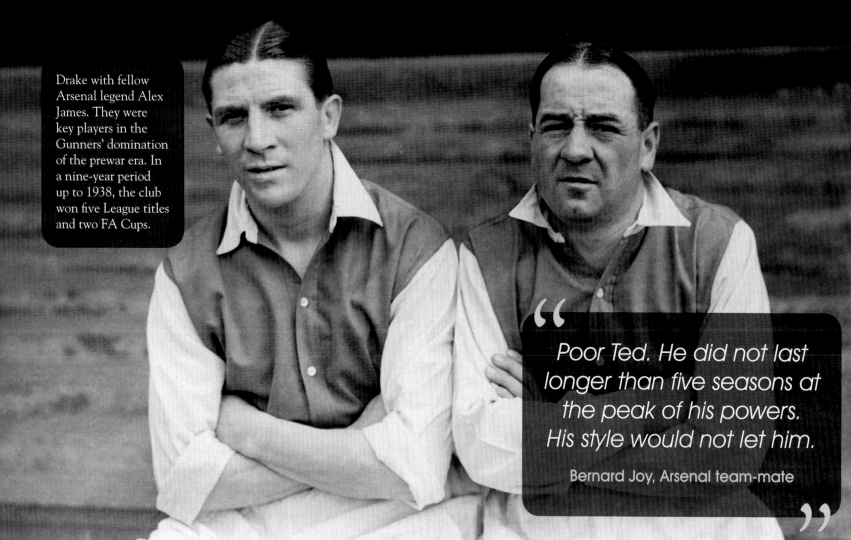

Drake with fellow Arsenal legend Alex James. They were key players in the Gunners' domination of the prewar era. In a nine-year period up to 1938, the club won five League titles and two FA Cups.

> "Poor Ted. He did not last longer than five seasons at the peak of his powers. His style would not let him."
>
> Bernard Joy, Arsenal team-mate

Football is littered with ifs and buts. What if Ted Drake had been signed by Spurs instead of their North London rivals? Had Tottenham not dithered over signing the then-injured schoolboy, the balance of power in North London might well have shifted. What is almost certain is that for any side Ted Drake would have scored goals – and plenty of them.

As one of the most prolific of all prewar goalscorers, Hampshire-born Drake (who played cricket for his home county) had an attack-minded philosophy which he stuck by throughout his career, as a player and a manager. His approach was not particularly sophisticated, but based on pace, power and a direct purpose, and it was superbly effective.

Taken on by his local club Southampton, he scored over a goal every two games at The Dell before Arsenal paid £6,500 to finally get him to make the move to the capital. It was at Highbury where Drake really made his name. He was instrumental in Arsenal's continuing success, as manager George Allison carried on the outstanding work of his predecessor Herbert Chapman, and maintained the Gunners' position as the best side in the land.

Drake's 139 goals came in just five seasons, and were fundamental to another three titles, most conspicuously with the 42 he scored during the 1934–35 League campaign that included an astonishing seven hat-tricks. He did not receive a medal for the 1933–34 triumph, having only played 10 games, but his seven goals that season were a key contributory factor in Arsenal's success.

He scored all seven in a 7-1 thrashing of Aston Villa in December 1935 despite carrying an injury – an indication of his bravery and toughness, and unequivocal proof of his phenomenal scoring rate. Drake was the archetypal centre-forward who was prepared to put his body on the line in his hungry pursuit of goals. His career was ended in 1945, owing to a legacy of injuries.

His playing days had also been interrupted by service in the RAF during the Second World War.

That was another "what if?" – what feats might Drake have achieved had he been able to continue playing when he was at his peak, rather than joining the fight against Hitler? It is a question that will never be answered. What was clear was that Drake still had much to offer the game. He served his managerial apprenticeship with Reading before taking over at Chelsea.

Chelsea was a club that had meandered along for 50 years without troubling the list of trophy winners, but Drake changed all that. He transformed the outlook of the club, injecting ambition and enthusiasm into a team of youngsters and previously unheralded pros. Drake's happy and confident nature was infectious, and Chelsea won the League against the odds in 1954–55, making him the first man to win the title as both a player and a manager.

The youth of his players prompted the nickname "Drake's Ducklings" for a Chelsea side which, while it did not win further trophies, did much to create the image of a club

Club	Appearances	Goals
Southampton	74	48
Arsenal	184	139

Country	Appearances	Goals
England	5	6
TOTAL	**263**	**193**

Honours

League Title	2 (1934–35, 1937–38)
FA Cup	1 (1936)
As a manager	1 League title (1954–55)

FOOTBALL —STATS—

Ted Drake

Name: Edward Joseph Drake
Born: Southampton, 16th August 1912
Died: 30th May 1995
Position: Striker
Playing career: 1931–45

that was to flourish in the Swinging Sixties and beyond. Drake was not there to oversee it – he had been sacked in 1961. In between stints as a bookmaker and insurance salesman, he took up a variety of posts at a colourful range of clubs, from Fulham to Barcelona, before his eventual retirement, during which he continued to watch and enjoy the game he gave so much service to.

LEFT: All aboard on England duty with Arsenal team-mates Cliff Bastin and Eddie Hapgood, Alf Young, Ken Willingham and Arsenal and England trainer Tom Whittaker. Drake's international appearances were limited by injury and then the war, but he made a big impact in his few outings. He scored the winner on his England debut and on home turf in the infamous Battle of Highbury against Italy.

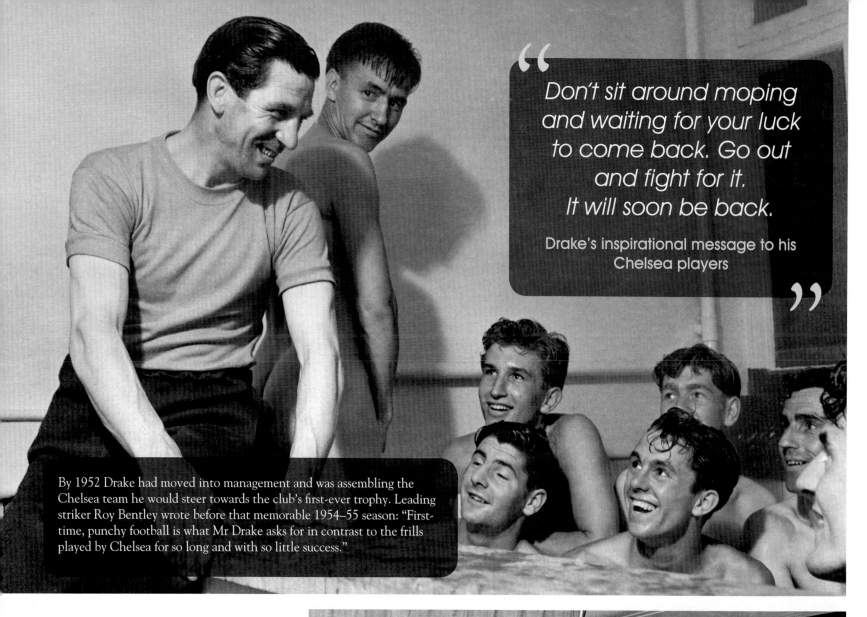

> *Don't sit around moping and waiting for your luck to come back. Go out and fight for it. It will soon be back.*
>
> Drake's inspirational message to his Chelsea players

By 1952 Drake had moved into management and was assembling the Chelsea team he would steer towards the club's first-ever trophy. Leading striker Roy Bentley wrote before that memorable 1954–55 season: "First-time, punchy football is what Mr Drake asks for in contrast to the frills played by Chelsea for so long and with so little success."

Having left Chelsea, Drake took up a variety of coaching positions, though many inside and outside the game felt his managerial talent was not appreciated or utilized as well as it could have been. Instead Drake brought his wisdom to the newly created Pools Panel in January 1963, joining Arthur Ellis, Tom Finney and Tommy Lawton to decide the outcome of matches called off during the big freeze that winter.

14

Stanley Matthews was a teetotaller, but made an exception for a celebratory drink from the FA Cup trophy.

STANLEY MATTHEWS

"The Wizard of the Dribble" . . . English football's first knight . . . "the First Gentleman of Soccer". Few footballers have – or will ever hope – to reach the standard set by Sir Stanley Matthews. Not just for playing the game, but in terms of character and enduring reputation.

There are not many footballers who have an FA Cup final named after them, but while the 1953 contest may be set down in the record books as a magnificent match between Blackpool and Bolton Wanderers, it will be forever known as the "Matthews Final".

The great man did not score for Blackpool in the pulsating 4-3 victory, but he was the one who utterly transformed it with one of the most extraordinary passages of play in the long history of the game.

At 3-1 down and with just 20 minutes to go, it looked like FA Cup glory would yet again elude Matthews (he had been a runner-up twice before). He was having none of it. In an electric series of dashes down the right flank he set up one goal for Stan Mortensen and then, after Mortensen had equalized, Matthews fashioned the winner for Bill Perry to seal an incredible comeback.

That the whole country (and even some Bolton fans) was pleased for Matthews says much about his appeal. He was the biggest draw of his day and would comfortably add 10,000 to a gate. 100,000 packed the streets for his funeral.

For a figure of such renown, Matthews emerged from typically humble origins but with a sense of decency and fair play instilled in him by his mother and father Jack, who was a former boxer. With football skills honed on the streets of Stoke, Matthews was signed up by his local club and stayed there for 15 years, though during this time his footballing career was interrupted by service in the RAF when he was stationed at Blackpool.

Matthews went on to join Blackpool, yet his character was out of step with that of his breezy, brassy adopted home. Quiet and reserved, he shunned the limelight. Pre-match nerves were a lifelong feature of his game, but once on the pitch and with a ball at his feet he found his stage and shone like the brightest of stars. Mercurial, dazzling, thrilling – all those superlatives and more were repeatedly used to describe Matthews' style of play. His burst of speed over short distances, unerring control and gift for creating a pass or a cross made him arguably the most lethal player in the English game.

He was not a prolific goalscorer, but as a provider of goals he was unsurpassed. Defenders knew what they were up against, yet were often powerless to do anything about it. The number of times Matthews feinted to cut in on the left only to swerve to the right and beat his man are near countless.

His long career straddled a number of eras: the prewar age of cloth-capped players and paltry wages; the postwar golden age of vast attendances feasting on the magic created by a roster of English greats; the end of the maximum wage and the long-overdue elevation of footballers to esteemed professionals with the rewards to match. Matthews played in front of Hitler in Berlin in 1938 where he was compelled to give the Nazi salute, was a friend of the Duke of Edinburgh, and won a whole generation of black fans in apartheid-era South Africa where he later coached in Soweto.

Club	Appearances	Goals
Stoke City	259	51
Blackpool	379	17
Stoke City	59	3

Country	Appearances	Goals
England	54	12
TOTAL	**751**	**83**

Honours

FA Cup   1 (1953)

FOOTBALL –STATS–

Stanley Matthews

Name: Stanley Matthews
Born: Hanley, 1st February 1915
Died: 23rd February 2000
Position: Outside-right
Playing career: 1932–65

Matthews (aloft, right) finally gets his hands on the FA Cup. He is seen here as a winner being carried by team-mates alongside his skipper Harry Johnston.

> "We were in awe of him . . . Matthews was a giant in our eyes.
>
> Ferenc Puskás

The longevity of this career was not simply down to innate talent but pure hard work. Matthews had an almost monastic approach to keeping himself fit and maintaining his lightning speed. He followed a punishing regime. He didn't drink or smoke, was virtually vegetarian, would go without food every Monday to keep his weight down and would stretch and push his body in training relentlessly. He was supremely dedicated and not one for socializing. Some saw this as aloofness, while others recognized and admired a man simply committed to his craft.

He was the first Footballer of the Year in 1948 and the oldest man to play for England at the age of 42. In 1956, Matthews (perhaps inevitably) became the first European Footballer of the Year. He rejoined Stoke in 1961 when most players of his age were already well into their retirement, and gates at the Victoria Ground quadrupled overnight. Knighted in 1965 – the first professional player ever to win the honour while still playing – he played his final game at 50 but still turned out for fun at 70!

A short-lived managerial career at Port Vale was not a success. Matthews was not a man without flaws: some team-mates resented his tendency not to pass and tackle. His unassuming, almost unemotional public image was belied by a passionate and long-lasting second marriage to Mila, who had been a low-level Czech spy. It was perhaps an unlikely love story for such an unassuming individual, but only adds to the allure of one of English football's most celebrated sons.

RIGHT INSET: Matthews' international fame and popularity ensured the world's greats were desperate to play in his testimonial in 1965. Welcoming Alfredo Di Stéfano (left) to Manchester's Ringway Airport, Sir Stan was also joined by Ferenc Puskás and László Kubala (on the right).

18

ABOVE: Stoke City fans welcome back their favourite son for a second stint in the Potteries. Fans of all persuasions worshipped Matthews. In an age of huge attendances he was the biggest draw, attracting many supporters simply so they could see him in thrilling action.

Players too gave their glowing respect. Nat Lofthouse once said of Sir Stan, "He stood there, toes turned inwards, looking like a little old man – until he moved." Joe Mercer called him "unplayable". Billy Wright complained that the England selectors had dropped the ageing Matthews too early. But the man himself? "I don't know if I was all that good. I never saw myself play, so how do I know?"

LEFT: That old Matthews magic. Southampton's Peter Sillett was just one of hundreds of defenders to be left flummoxed by Matthews' wing wizardry, 1953.

> " Soccer has been good to me . . . "

TOM FINNEY

Preston born and bred, revered and commemorated by the Lancashire town, Tom Finney was the embodiment of the one-club man. As well as serving his birthplace and country with the utmost distinction, he was one of Britain's greatest players.

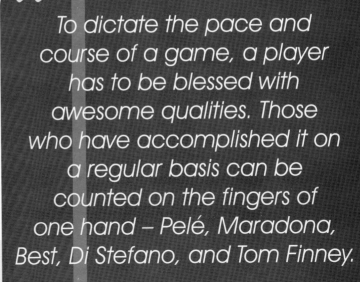

> "To dictate the pace and course of a game, a player has to be blessed with awesome qualities. Those who have accomplished it on a regular basis can be counted on the fingers of one hand – Pelé, Maradona, Best, Di Stefano, and Tom Finney."
>
> Sir Stanley Matthews

When **FOOTBALL** *Was* **FOOTBALL**

Still making a splash. Floral and club-colour tributes surround the famous statue of Sir Tom Finney outside his beloved Deepdale, marking his passing at the age of 91 in 2014.

For such an iconic player, Tom Finney had a late start in sporting life. The Second World War meant the fast-paced winger had to pull on battle fatigues and drive a tank in the North African desert and Italy before he could don the lilywhite first-team shirt of Preston North End. He was 24 when he made his debut, but with potentially half of his career already gone, he set about making up for lost time.

Left-footed by nature, he could play on either flank. He was a fantastic dribbler, fast – and despite his relatively small stature – outstanding in the air. Finney had so much variety to his game that by the time he had retired he had played in every one of the five forward positions and was world-class in each of them.

A mainstay of the England national side, he earned the enduring respect of his peers who readily recognized the sheer depth of his talent. Former Preston team-mate Bill Shankly rated Finney as the best player ever born. Centre-forwards loved him for the goalscoring opportunities he presented to them on a plate. Stanley Matthews, his great rival for the coveted right-wing berth with England, was a firm friend; when the two played together in the national side, Finney simply switched to the left.

Once, after the second of two emphatic wins over Portugal, the defeated team rose as one at the post-match banquet to toast Finney, hailing him as "the master". Finney's renown was global.

But it was at Preston that people really took Finney to their hearts. Few have made such an indelible mark on one club than the man born just a street away from Deepdale. He in turn had a road named after him, and a stand with his face picked out in white amid the bank of blue seats.

A statue outside captures Finney in one of his most famous settings. Sliding through a puddle and sending a shower of water into the air, it's called "The Splash", and is based on a photograph taken during a game at Chelsea in 1956. It evokes

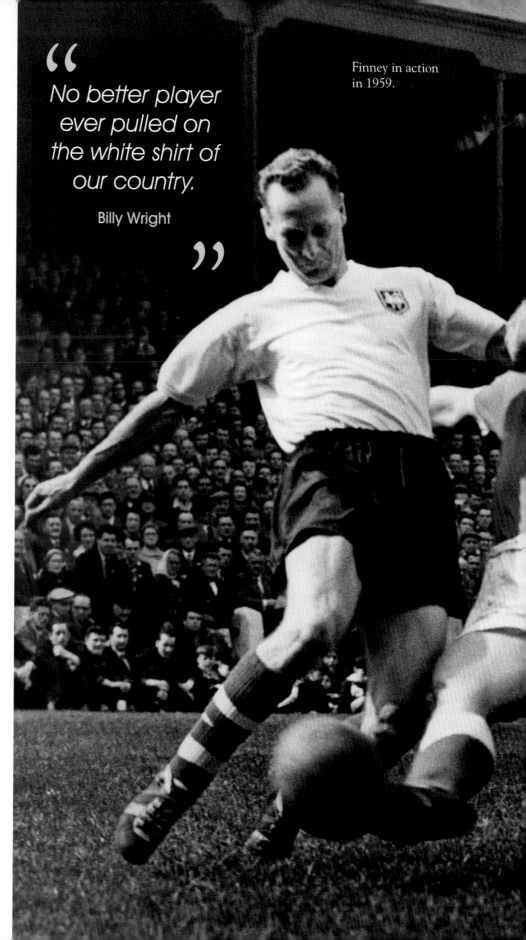

"
No better player ever pulled on the white shirt of our country.

Billy Wright

"

Finney in action in 1959.

the athleticism, poise and immaculate technique that Finney brought to his game.

The reason for such enduring celebration of his life is simple. Finney was not just a brilliant footballer – one of the genuine all-time greats – but a loyal, dignified and warm-hearted gentleman loved and admired by all who met him. He was dubbed the "Preston Plumber" on account of serving an apprenticeship in the family business before he turned pro, and a telling indicator of his modest approach to life.

Club	Appearances	Goals
Preston North End	473	210
Country	Appearances	Goals
England	76	30
TOTAL	549	240

FOOTBALL –STATS–

Tom Finney

Name: Thomas Finney
Born: Preston, 5th April 1922
Died: 14th February 2014
Position: Winger
Playing career: 1946–60

He had offers to play elsewhere, notably with Palermo in Italy, enticed by a jaw-dropping signing on fee of £10,000 and riches far beyond anything he could earn in England in those maximum-wage days of £12 a week. The club swiftly blocked any such move, but Finney was not bitter. He remained at heart a Preston man. It probably cost him honours. Twice the club were runners-up in the League and were losing FA Cup finalists in 1954, but the lack of silverware did not diminish Finney's lustre. Asked what was the highlight of his career, he answered "staying with Preston".

After his playing days ended, he became club president and played an active role in the community. Knighted in 1998, he had a ready smile and wave for anyone who had the privilege of passing him on the street. To the end, Finney was a Preston man.

Finney put the football world to rights alongside Joe Mercer and former Preston team-mate Bill Shankly during the "Bless 'Em All" Week at Pontins in Blackpool.

RIGHT: Part of the measure of Finney's influence in Preston is that his presence has been made permanent in and around Deepdale, especially with this street named in his honour.

BELOW: Arriving at Euston station and accompanying the wives and girlfriends of his successors in the Preston team for the 1964 FA Cup final. Sadly, just like Finney, they ended up on the losing side, going down 3-2 to West Ham.

> " Aye, they're as good as Tommy now – but then Tommy's over 60. "
>
> Bill Shankly, when asked to compare players of the late 1970s with Finney

24

Lofthouse scores the first of his two goals that secured the 1958 FA Cup final victory for Bolton Wanderers.

NAT LOFTHOUSE

Like his contemporary and great England colleague Tom Finney, Nat Lofthouse was a dedicated one-club man and a national hero, celebrated for his bravery and all-action style.

When FOOTBALL *Was* FOOTBALL

Not many 15-year-old boys can cope with pressure of a first-team debut at such a tender age. But then Nat Lofthouse was no ordinary teenager. Plunged into the hurly-burly of a local derby against Lancashire rivals Bury, the youngster scored two goals in a 5-1 wartime win. A local legend who would become a national icon was born.

In truth, Lofthouse took time to properly settle at Bolton, but once established he became a rampaging centre-forward who struck fear into defenders at home and abroad. While he was not tall, at only 5ft 9in, he was strong as a bull – a physicality that had stemmed from work as a Bevin Boy down the mines during the Second World War, hauling tubs of coal from four in the morning before training with Bolton in the afternoon.

With hostilities at an end, Lofthouse put that strength to productive use leading the Wanderers' line. There was nothing fancy about his style. He could be a blunt instrument when charging goalkeepers or hurtling into challenges. But he was fast, powerful, adept in the air and there was dynamite in both his boots.

Having flourished in the early postwar years, he earned his first England call-up in 1950. It was with the national side that Lofthouse enjoyed some of his finest hours.

He scored twice on his debut in a 2-2 draw with Yugoslavia, before giving a career-defining display against a highly talented Austria in 1952. He had already scored once as the teams were deadlocked at 2-2. Then, with nine minutes to go, Tom Finney set Lofthouse free to break away and notch the

After being on the losing side in the classic 1953 "Matthews Final", Lofthouse finally got his hands on the coveted trophy five years later.

> "He was not only a great player, he was a great character."
>
> Don Howe

winner. He charged from just inside his own half and slotted home as the hosts' goalkeeper crashed into the Englishman, knocking him clean out. Lofthouse came to, returned to the fray and was held aloft by British servicemen in the crowd who had spilled on to the pitch. Their hero was soon dubbed "The Lion of Vienna", and the name stuck.

Lofthouse scored a remarkable 30 goals in just 33 games for England, one of the most prolific ratios in the history of the side. So it was met with great bewilderment when he was dropped from the 1958 World Cup squad by the amateur selectors who at the time picked the players.

Compensation came in the 1958 FA Cup final when Lofthouse scored both goals in a 2-0 win over Manchester United. That it came so soon after the Munich air disaster, and that the second was the result of Lofthouse crudely barging United keeper Harry Gregg over the line hardly endeared the Bolton man to neutrals. It was a legitimate

Club	Appearances	Goals
Bolton Wanderers	503	285
Country	Appearances	Goals
England	33	30
TOTAL	**536**	**315**

Honours	
FA Cup	1 (1958)

FOOTBALL —STATS—

Nat Lofthouse

Name: Nathaniel Lofthouse
Born: Bolton, 27th August 1925
Died: 15th January 2011
Position: Centre-forward
Playing career: 1946–60

tactic at the time but not a popular one. Still, it typified the striker's wholehearted commitment.

This was never better illustrated than in his unstinting service of his beloved Bolton. He stayed on at the club after retirement from playing in 1960, enduring an unhappy spell as manager between 1968 and 1970, but stepping in as caretaker boss three times, in between a variety of other roles at the club he devoted his life to.

Nat's marriage to his beloved Alma lasted nearly 40 years. She sadly passed away in 1985.

Belgium were on the end of a Lofthouse belter in a November 1952 international at Wembley. The Bolton man scored twice in a 5-0 thrashing.

" *We're a first division club in every sense of the word.*

Lofthouse on Bolton when he was the club's president "

Lofthouse's passing moved fans of all generations – even those too young to have seen him play.

BILLY WRIGHT

Billy Wright spanned the eras between the golden age of the 1950s and the new era of the celebrity footballer. Over a stellar career he was the rock around which two sides – his club and his country – were built.

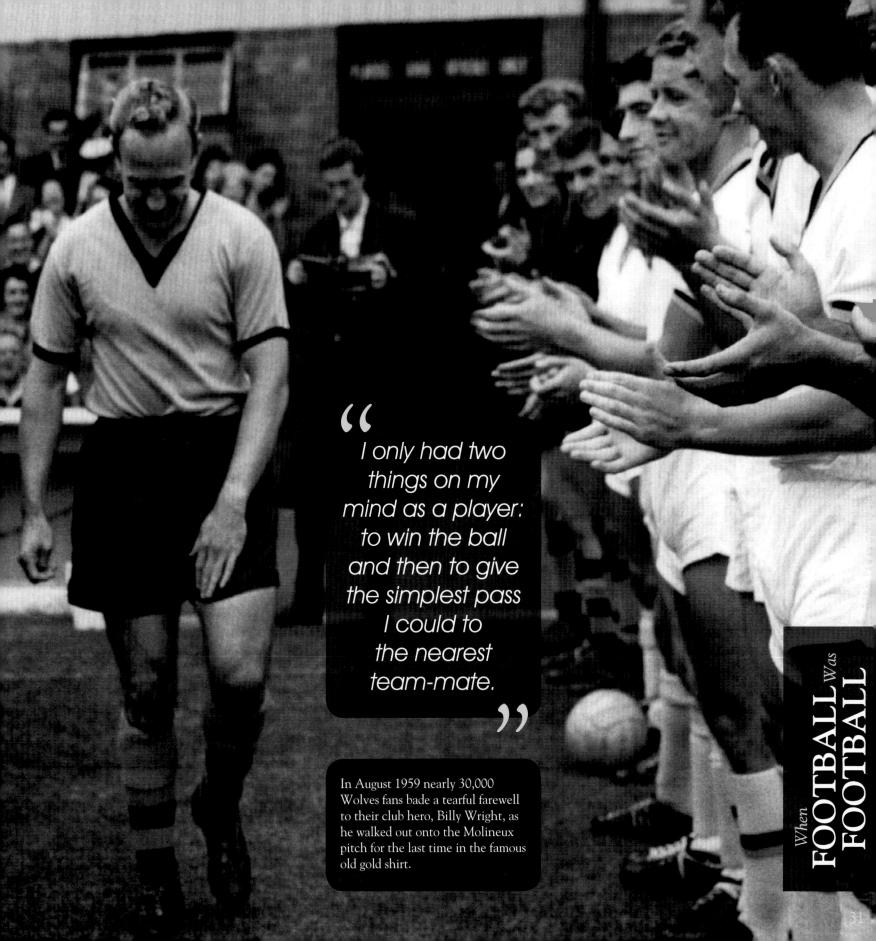

> " *I only had two things on my mind as a player: to win the ball and then to give the simplest pass I could to the nearest team-mate.* "

In August 1959 nearly 30,000 Wolves fans bade a tearful farewell to their club hero, Billy Wright, as he walked out onto the Molineux pitch for the last time in the famous old gold shirt.

In many respects Billy Wright was the most traditional of English footballing heroes. He was old enough to have served during the Second World War, played for just one club, was never booked or dismissed throughout a 20-year career and featured in nearly 700 games.

Yet he was something of a trailblazer as well. He was one of the stars of early floodlit games against foreign opposition that broadened traditionally limited English horizons; he was a celebrity footballer with a wife – Joy Beverley – who was famous in her own right; and in retirement he moved into the media as a television executive. To some extent the story of Wright was the story of football over seven decades.

That tale began in 1924 among the heavy industry of the Shropshire iron works. The young Wright emerged from this environment, showing prodigious talent as a striker. While Wolves manager Major Frank Buckley initially felt Wright was too small to make it in the pro ranks, the youth was given a chance and, by 1939, Wright had switched to defence and made his first-team debut. When his career resumed in peacetime, Wright was swiftly called up for national football service – making the first of over a century of full England internationals.

Made captain in 1948, he skippered the side for a record-equalling 90 matches. At the heart of the England defence he was an inspirational leader – setting the example with ceaseless effort, perfectly timed and executed tackles and a near-flawless ability to read the game. Nearly flawless because he – and the rest of the team – were embarrassingly exposed by the brilliant Hungarians in two humiliating defeats in 1953 and 1954.

Those reverses were more than compensated for, however, by the glittering successes. Wright played in three World Cups as English football at last embraced international competition, but he only earned actual trophy success with Wolves. The dominant team of the 1950s under the enlightened management of Stan Cullis, they won three League titles during Wright's captaincy. Friendly matches against the likes of Honvéd and Dynamo Moscow did much to usher in the age of European club football, especially at a time when the game's authorities were determined that English sides would not participate in such contests. Wolves – and Wright – showed what a thrilling spectacle midweek football played at night against exotic opposition could be.

After 20 years in the Black Country, in 1959 Wright finally called it a day to huge adulation from fans around the country. He moved into management, but not with success. His four-year tenure as Arsenal boss was an indifferent one, as he struggled to make the transition from the ultimate team player to the governor who had to lay down the law. However, a new career as head of sport at ATV and Central represented a daring change from the familiar tale of "ex-player runs pub". It was not all happiness, though – the pressures of work led to a drink problem but, by 1989, Wright was back at Molineux, installed as a director of the club for which he had been such a magnificent player.

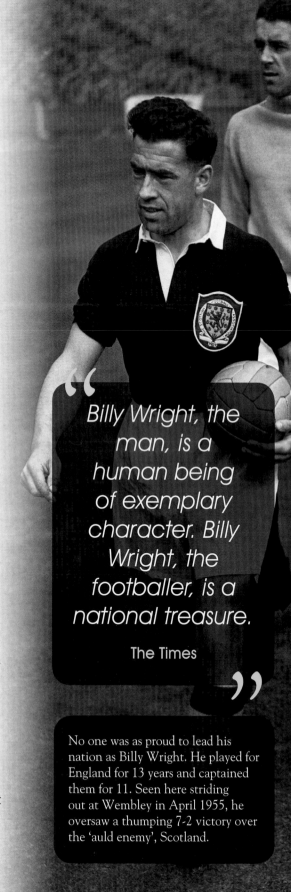

"

Billy Wright, the man, is a human being of exemplary character. Billy Wright, the footballer, is a national treasure.

The Times

"

No one was as proud to lead his nation as Billy Wright. He played for England for 13 years and captained them for 11. Seen here striding out at Wembley in April 1955, he oversaw a thumping 7-2 victory over the 'auld enemy', Scotland.

Club	Appearances	Goals
Wolverhampton Wanderers	541	16
Country	Appearances	Goals
England	105	3
TOTAL	**646**	**19**

Honours

League Title	3 (1953–54, 1957–58, 1958–59)
FA Cup	1 (1949)

BELOW: Slightly pained smiles with Nándor Hidegkuti in 1953 – but the Hungarian and his team-mates had just given Wright and England the complete runaround in a humbling 6-3 thrashing. The loss – and a 7-1 follow-up less than a year later in Budapest – prompted much soul-searching within English football.

FOOTBALL –STATS–

Billy Wright

Name: William Ambrose Wright
Born: Ironbridge, 6th February 1924
Died: 3rd September 1994
Position: Centre-half
Playing career: 1939–59

RIGHT: Wright's relationship with and marriage to Joy Beverley, one of the famous Beverley Sisters, made the couple the Posh and Becks of their day. They were greeted by press photographers eager to capture Joy's tender welcome for Billy at London Airport, as he returned from the 1958 World Cup in Sweden.

> **"**
> *When you trained or played with him, as I did from the age of 17, it felt that here was a man upon whom you wanted to model yourself.*
> *Every player had respect for Billy.*
> **"**
>
> Ron Flowers

ABOVE: Showing the poise and technique that made Wright such an accomplished defender.

BELOW: Domestic bliss: even the most famous footballers had to light their own fires in 1951.

> **"**
> *I noticed the Hungarians had these strange lightweight boots, like slippers. I turned to Stan Mortensen and said 'We should be alright here, they haven't got the proper kit.'*
> **"**

Despite signing big-name players like Joe Baker in 1962, Wright struggled to make the transition from a playing career to one in the management. The famous clock at the Clock End at Highbury was ticking down on Wright's four years in the Arsenal job.

I'm not equipped to manage successfully without him. I'm the shop front, he is the goods at the back.

Clough on Peter Taylor

Cups that cheer: Peter Taylor (left) and Brian Clough celebrate the point gained from a 0-0 draw with Coventry City at Highfield Road that won Nottingham Forest the 1977–78 League title. Clough and Taylor were one of the great managerial double acts. Taylor publicly played the perfect role of sidekick to the extrovert Clough, but he was fundamental to the success the pair enjoyed. They did not always get on – there were serious and ultimately enduring rifts – but the teams they produced rank among the best English football has seen.

BRIAN CLOUGH

Is there any other man who has made such a mark on the English game as Brian Clough? While he rightly made his reputation as one of the great – if not the greatest – managers, he was also a wonderful player whose career was cruelly cut short by injury.

When FOOTBALL *Was* FOOTBALL

Over a decade after his death, the shadow of Brian Clough still looms large over English football. Every time the national side fails, memories of Clough, "the best manager England never had" are rekindled. Every time a club season is dominated by the same powerful sides, fans talk wistfully of the days when Clough took a comparatively small provincial outfit to European Cup glory.

Arguably the most compelling individual ever to play, manage or simply talk about the game, Clough forged the bulk of his reputation in managing such sides as Nottingham Forest and Derby County. But his achievements with the East Midlands rivals, coupled with his outspoken image, tend to overshadow his career as a footballer – for he was a truly outstanding player.

The sixth of nine children born to an injured First World War veteran who worked in a sweet factory, and a mother he adored, Clough signed for his home-town club of Middlesbrough. Despite early doubts on the part of the coaches, he emerged as one of the great English prospects. He was a natural goalscorer and soon established a prodigious record. In just five seasons he rattled in 197 League goals in just 213 appearances. He never scored less than 36 in a season.

These came in the Second Division, but Boro were not progressing to nearly the same extent as their striker. Clough was clearly destined to play for a club with ambitions to match his. His talent and his character demanded it. When he was made captain, his team-mates at Ayresome Park objected. They didn't take to Clough's single-minded determination, his professionalism and his outspoken ways. Sunderland, however, were desperate to get back into the top flight and eager to see if they could cope with this larger-than-life character, and so the Wearsiders bought Clough for a fee of £45,000.

At Roker Park Clough was equally prolific, scoring 63 goals in just 74 appearances. But the limited number of games he participated in told its own story. In a Boxing Day match against Bury, Clough was involved in a sickening collision with opposition goalkeeper Chris Harker, as the Sunderland striker charged through on goal on a rain-slicked pitch. The clash wrought havoc on Clough's knee ligaments and he was unable to stand. After two years of punishing rehabilitation, Clough made an attempt at a playing comeback – but it was no use. In the days before the kind of medical advances that could rebuild shattered knees, Clough's playing days were over.

It was a devastating blow. He took another year to get over the setback and turned to drink, which would prove such a burden to his life decades later. But, teaming up with his old Middlesbrough colleague Peter Taylor at Hartlepool, he set in train a managerial career that

The 23-year-old Clough in familiar penalty-area action for his home-town club Middlesbrough.

"
We knew it was hopeless, but we couldn't tell him because it would have shattered him.

Alan Brown, Clough's manager at Sunderland on seeing the extent of the injury
"

Club	Appearances	Goals
Middlesbrough	222	204
Sunderland	74	63

Country	Appearances	Goals
England	2	0
TOTAL	**298**	**267**

Honours (as a manager)

League Title	2 (1971–72 Derby; 1977–78 Nottingham Forest)
European Cup	2 (1978–79, 1979–80, Nottingham Forest)
League Cup	4 (1977–78, 1978–79, 1988–89, 1989–90, Nottingham Forest)

LEFT: Clough in action for Sunderland against Bury on 26th December 1962. Just moments later he suffered the dreadful knee injury that would end his brilliant playing career.

FOOTBALL –STATS–

Brian Clough

Name: Brian Howard Clough
Born: Middlesbrough, 21st March 1935
Died: 20th September 2004
Position: Centre-forward
Playing career: 1955–64

For once, Clough is in the background (centre), as the greats of the game gather to pay tribute to former Sheffield United and England star, Jimmy Hagan (standing, signing a ball). Playing in his testimonial for an All-Star XI in March 1958 were Tom Finney, Bert Trautmann (seated), Stanley Matthews, Danny Blanchflower, Jimmy McIlroy, Bill McGarry, Alf McMichael, Jimmy Armfield and Bob McKinlay.

was to transcend any disappointments he suffered as a player. Clough's playing days were a case of "what might have been"; as a manager he would be a greater success than even the biggest fans of this most confident and extrovert of men could have imagined.

Together, Clough and Taylor transformed the fortunes of Derby County, taking them to a League title in 1971–72. After a year with Brighton, Clough's solo stint at Leeds United was a 44-day disaster, but, reunited with Taylor at Nottingham Forest, he created one of the most romantic of all football success stories, taking the side from Second Division obscurity to the pinnacle of the club game and to two European Cup triumphs. It was a phenomenal achievement that would be almost impossible today.

It took its toll and, allied to the ravages of alcoholism and associated ill-health, ended Clough's life at 69. But what a life it had been.

ABOVE: Key to Clough's genius as a manager was his ability to take unheralded or underachieving players and mould them into brilliant individuals who could function superbly in a team. Kenny Burns was a case in point – he switched from his striker role to become an excellent centre-half at the City Ground.

LEFT: Clough senior with Clough junior, future England, Liverpool and Nottingham Forest star, Nigel. Nigel's older brother Simon can be seen in the background, peeping through the door.

"
We talk about it for twenty minutes
and then we decide I was right.

Brian Clough
"

RIGHT: Clough was a media natural, who often had a better grasp of a story or a good quote than his journalistic inquisitors. He had a good relationship with ITV's long-time football commentator and presenter, Brian Moore.

BELOW: The football man: Clough is seen here in 1975 getting proceedings under way in the ancient annual Shrove Tuesday and Ash Wednesday football match in Ashbourne, Derbyshire.

The 20-year-old Johnny Haynes in pre-season training.

JOHNNY HAYNES

He was known as the "£100 a week man" – the footballer who broke the outdated maximum wage to receive pay approaching his true worth – but there was much more to this elegant and gifted player.

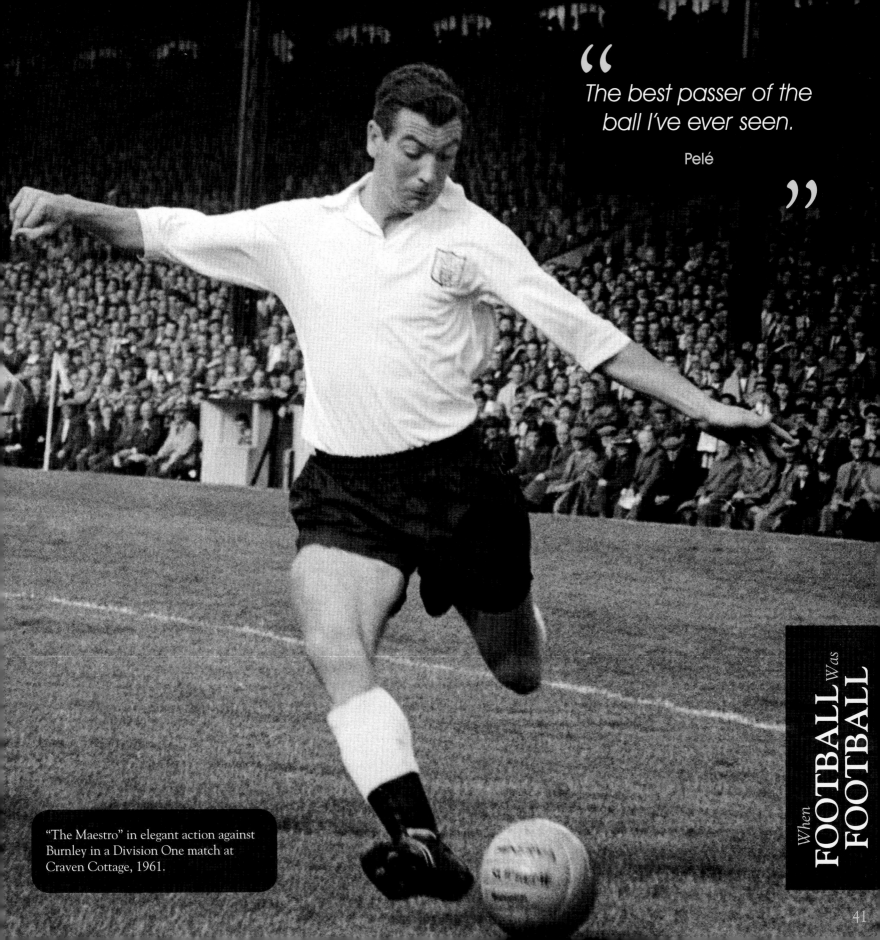

> " The best passer of the ball I've ever seen.
>
> Pelé "

"The Maestro" in elegant action against Burnley in a Division One match at Craven Cottage, 1961.

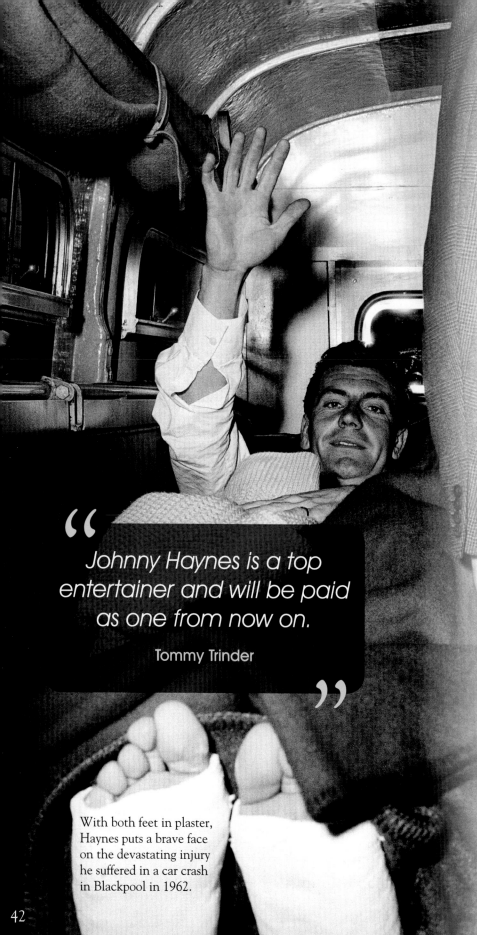

> **Johnny Haynes is a top entertainer and will be paid as one from now on.**
>
> Tommy Trinder

With both feet in plaster, Haynes puts a brave face on the devastating injury he suffered in a car crash in Blackpool in 1962.

In the hurly-burly world of mid-1950s English football when great players often needed brawn to compete, the young Johnny Haynes stood out. He was graceful, balanced and precise. His passing was exemplary, his goals often spectacular and his range of skills showcased him as a refined footballer perhaps better suited to a less rudimentary, more technical style of football. In the 1960s and with a new, less robust kind of game developing, he would probably have flourished even more had it not been for a car accident that restricted his talent.

What if he had not broken both feet in the accident on Blackpool seafront in 1962? What if it hadn't caused him to miss a whole season? What if he had been able to prolong what had been a hitherto successful England career?

It might have been Johnny Haynes rather than Bobby Moore leading England out for the final of the World Cup in 1966. Haynes (the first player to feature for England at all levels) had already captained the side 22 times and orchestrated one of the most entertaining spells the Three Lions ever enjoyed, with 40 goals scored between 1960 and 1961, including a 9-3 victory over Scotland.

World Cup success was elusive. In two campaigns (1958 and 1962) the legacy of long and tiring domestic seasons hampered England's progress. But Haynes was central to a more expansive, less inhibited England, and it provided him with the elite stage in contrast to that of his domestic football.

Another one-club man, Haynes stayed loyal to Fulham. At the time they were a popular and welcoming outfit whose chairman was comedian Tommy Trinder, but at the same time they were hardly likely to challenge for trophies. For the majority of Haynes' 18 years at the club, Fulham competed in the Second Division. Two losing FA Cup semi-finals and one promotion to Division One was scant reward for Haynes' artistry.

The Craven Cottage crowd greatly appreciated his loyalty. He was by some distance the club's best-ever player, and the lifting of the wage ceiling was in part due to the temptations that were being placed in Haynes' lap by foreign clubs like AC Milan, who recognized and coveted his skills. Haynes was good – very good

Club	Appearances	Goals
Fulham	657	157
Country	Appearances	Goals
England	56	18
TOTAL	**713**	**175**

BELOW: "You lucky people!": Fulham's star player with club chairman and comedian Tommy Trinder. Trinder had once joked that Haynes deserved £100 a week. With the lifting of the maximum wage, that quip came true.

FOOTBALL –STATS–

Johnny Haynes

Name: John Norman Haynes
Born: Kentish Town, London, 17th October 1934
Died: 18th October 2005
Position: Inside-forward
Playing career: 1952–70

– and he knew it. It was his Fulham team-mate Jimmy Hill who campaigned for the change, and the dashing inside-forward took advantage.

Good-looking, charismatic and nicknamed "The Maestro", he was a natural as the face of Brylcreem. Despite being dropped by Alf Ramsey when he took over as England boss, Haynes retained star appeal. He nearly moved back to the North London stomping grounds of his childhood in a transfer to Spurs, but Fulham blocked his way.

How would Haynes have fared in a team embodying the new age of fluent football? A case of "what if". But if Haynes was bitter, it didn't show. He stuck around in West London until 1970, by which time Fulham had dropped down to the Third Division. A long spell coaching in South Africa and success as a bookmaker was followed by a return to the UK in 1984 and retirement in Edinburgh with his third wife, Avril.

It was another car accident that ended his life, Haynes suffering a stroke at the wheel. He was 71.

LEFT: Haynes was a stylish perfectionist – even in a bowling alley.

BELOW: Captain Haynes meets the Duke of Edinburgh before kick-off in England's meeting with Scotland at Wembley on 15th April 1961. Haynes was the inspiration behind a 9-3 humiliation of the Scots. In truth it was a fairly tight game until the final 30 minutes, when England ran riot.

"In those last 20-odd minutes we just couldn't do anything wrong, almost supernatural, everything we tried ended up in the back of the net. We'd have beaten any team in history in that last half-hour.

Johnny Haynes on the 9-3 win over Scotland"

Duncan Edwards photographed shortly before the Munich air disaster. He and seven other members of the Manchester United team lost their lives.

DUNCAN EDWARDS

Manchester United, English football and the wider game was robbed of one of its most shining talents when Duncan Edwards died in the Munich air disaster. Nearly 60 years on from that terrible day, he still ranks among the true greats, even though his career was tragically cut short.

When FOOTBALL Was FOOTBALL

The common image of Duncan Edwards is of a youthful giant who towered over his contemporaries, not just in terms of literal stature but in reputation. The former is not quite true. He was big, but not conspicuously so. The latter, however, is more certain.

Edwards was the prodigy, the superstar, the future of the sport. He was powerful, strong and determined, with an iron will to win, but also skilful and blessed with a delicate touch, as befitted a boy who was, of all things, a folk dancer as a youth. Edwards led opponents a merry jig around the field over an all-too-brief but glorious five-year career.

Edwards was born in Dudley, but despite interest from local side Wolves had his heart set on Manchester United. He made his debut in 1953 as one of a number of youth-team players introduced by Matt Busby to inject vigour and dynamism into the team. As such Edwards was the natural leader of a group that would be christened the "Busby Babes".

He led by example, amazing seasoned pros, trainers and managers with his all-round ability. Jimmy Murphy, United's famous coach who did much of the groundwork to sow and nurture the various young talents that made up the Babes, saw Edwards as the clear superstar. Edwards had everything and more.

He displayed the mark of greatness early on and was soon called up to the national side at the age of just 18. The youngster went on to play a full part in two League title wins as Busby's team clicked into thrilling gear, and a dazzling career for both club and country beckoned. Then came Munich.

In the midst of United's trailblazing European Cup campaigns, Edwards had been a pivotal figure. In the second campaign United were maturing and looked as if they might lift the trophy. When the awful accident occurred amid the snow of Munich in February 1958, the loss of eight players and 15 others (including eight journalists) saddened not only United fans but the whole sport. A glimmer of hope came with the news that Edwards was clinging to life. His legs were shattered and his kidneys all but destroyed, but with customary bravery and an unquenchable will, he was battling to pull through.

It appeared at one stage he would survive – perhaps never to play football again, but at least to live. He had spoken to Bobby Charlton in his hospital bed and seemed to be rallying. He even talked about United's fixtures, concerned how the team might fare and apologetic for his absence. But the internal injuries finally got the better of him. He died 15 days after the crash. Because the collective hope that he would live was so despairingly extinguished, it made the tragedy all the crueller.

Edwards had been brilliant. He could have been even better – arguably the greatest, bar none. Subsequent United players who come through the ranks are often described as "the new Duncan Edwards" but it is an unfair comparison. He was unique and there will likely never be another to match him.

> *He was so good; when he was around you thought anything was possible.*
>
> Bobby Charlton

Club	Appearances	Goals
Manchester United	177	21
Country	Appearances	Goals
England	18	5
TOTAL	**195**	**26**
Honours		
League Title	2 (1955–56, 1956–57)	

FOOTBALL
–STATS–

Duncan Edwards

Name: Duncan Edwards

Born: Dudley, 1st October 1936

Died: 21st February 1958

Position: Left-half

Playing career: 1953–58

Forging through the mud and muck of English League football in 1957, Edwards is challenged by Aston Villa keeper Nigel Sims.

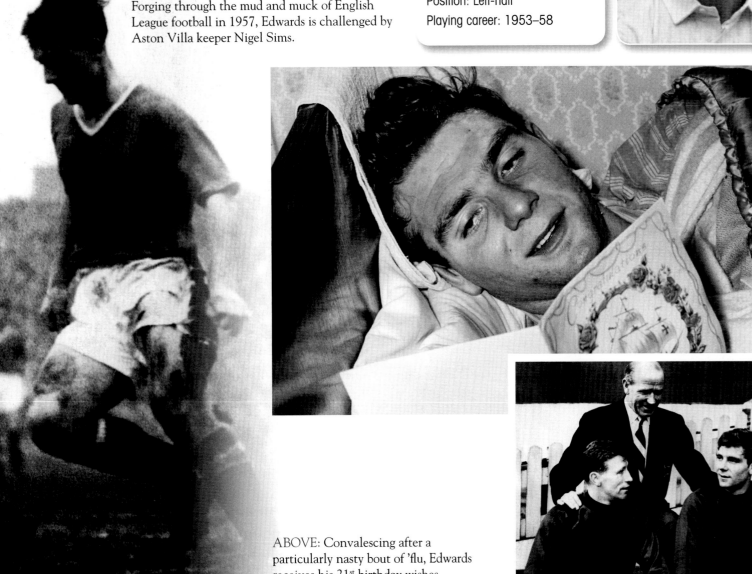

ABOVE: Convalescing after a particularly nasty bout of 'flu, Edwards receives his 21st birthday wishes.

RIGHT: Matt Busby lays a paternal hand on the shoulder of Edwards (right) and his fellow youthful Red Roger Byrne.

LEFT: Five of the Babes: Johnny Berry, Duncan Edwards, Mark Jones, Roger Byrne and Dennis Viollet.

BELOW: Superstar he may have been, but Edwards had to go through the same rigorous apprenticeship and living arrangements as any other young player. Seen here at Mrs Watson's famous Old Trafford guest house were (clockwise, from bottom left): Tommy Taylor, Mrs Watson, Bobby Charlton, Bill Whelan, Winnie, Jackie Blanchflower, Mark Jones, Gordon Clayton, Joan, Alan Rhodes and Duncan Edwards.

> " He remained an unspoiled boy to the end, his head the same size it had been from the start.
>
> Jimmy Murphy "

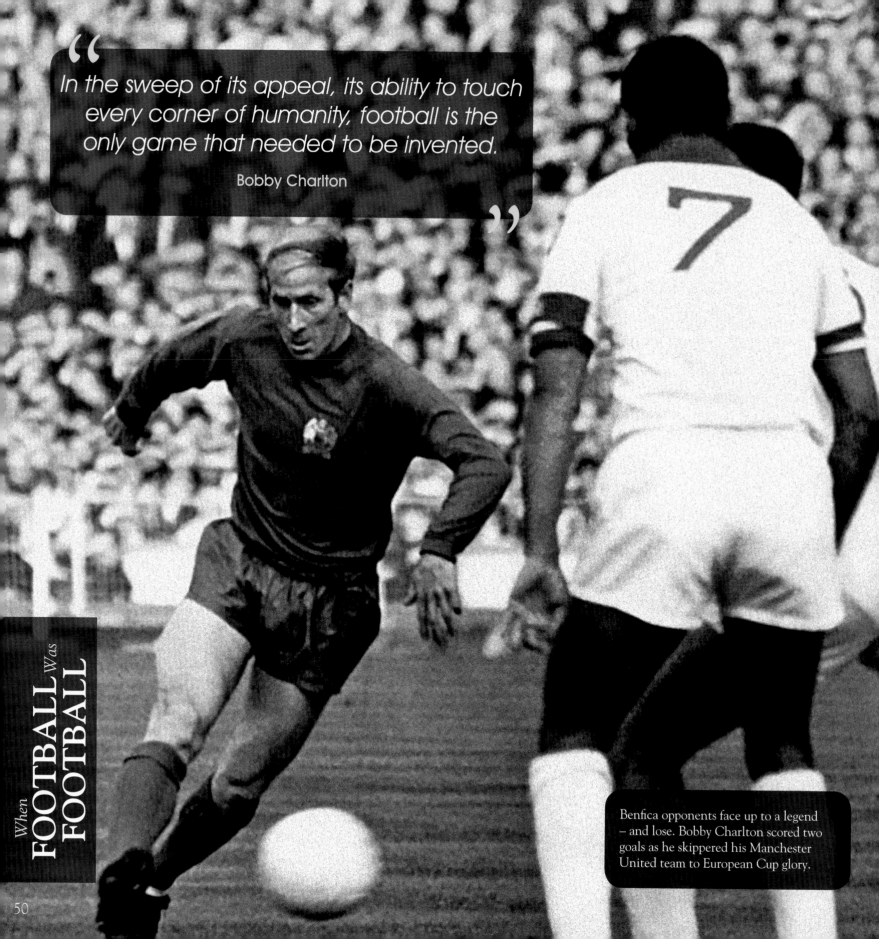

> *In the sweep of its appeal, its ability to touch every corner of humanity, football is the only game that needed to be invented.*
>
> Bobby Charlton

When
FOOTBALL *Was*
FOOTBALL

Benfica opponents face up to a legend – and lose. Bobby Charlton scored two goals as he skippered his Manchester United team to European Cup glory.

BOBBY CHARLTON

Arguably the most enduringly famous of all English players, Bobby Charlton is renowned and respected around the world, not only for his sporting achievements but for his character as a true gentleman of the game.

When football fans from different countries meet, any language divide is often overcome by a beer or two and by reciting the names of famous footballers. Pelé naturally gets a mention, as does Maradona, and it's safe to assume that Bobby Charlton will also be pronounced to much agreement.

Charlton is one of those footballers whose fame transcends what he did on the football field. He was an outstanding player for a generation, his longevity serving as evidence of the depth of his talent. He was the central figure in teams that took on the toughest opposition and won the greatest prizes. In retirement he is one of the sport's finest ambassadors, representing much that is good about the game.

He was raised as a street footballer in the north-east, coming from a production line that churned out a succession of wonderful players. His mother Cissie was not just a maternal influence but a formative sporting one as well – she would kick a ball around with him and brother Jack in the terraces of Ashington. Word soon spread in the area that there was a precociously gifted, small, blonde-haired boy who played phenomenal football, and that in turn led talent spotters from further afield to come calling. Manchester United's enviable scouting network secured his signature and Charlton headed to Old Trafford.

In time he became a United legend. He first came to prominence as one of the "Busby Babes". While he incurred relatively light injuries in the Munich air disaster, the experience had an understandably devastating effect on him. He lost good friends and would be haunted by the experience for the rest of his life, but the character he showed to come back and play even better in his team-mates' honour earned him adulation at Old Trafford and widespread respect and admiration.

He played with determination and a huge will to win, but also integrity. Charlton represented old-fashioned values of sportsmanship, respect and honesty, but was a thoroughly modern

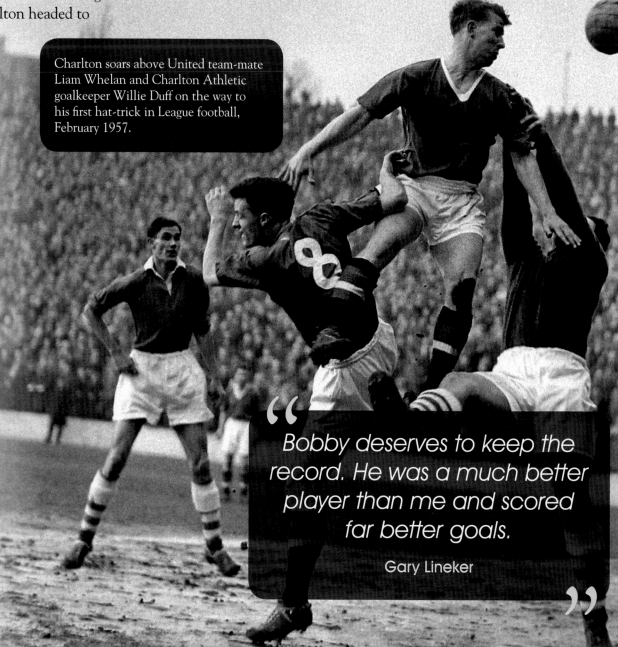

Charlton soars above United team-mate Liam Whelan and Charlton Athletic goalkeeper Willie Duff on the way to his first hat-trick in League football, February 1957.

> "Bobby deserves to keep the record. He was a much better player than me and scored far better goals."
>
> Gary Lineker

Club	Appearances	Goals
Manchester United	758	249
Preston North End	45	10

Country	Appearances	Goals
England	106	49
TOTAL	**909**	**308**

Honours

League Title	3 (1956–57, 1964–65, 1966–67)
FA Cup	1 (1962–63)
European Cup	1 (1967–68)
World Cup	1 (1966)

Bobby Charlton

Name: Robert Charlton
Born: Ashington, 11th October 1937
Position: Forward
Playing career: 1956–76

player. A deep-lying forward, he could drop into midfield to make thrilling runs on goal before unleashing scorching shots. A long-range Charlton netbuster became one of the most evocative images in 1960s football.

With George Best and Denis Law he formed one of the most effective trios the game has ever seen, as Busby's rebuilt side conquered all and sundry. The team's finest hour came in the 1968 European Cup when United, with Charlton scoring twice, became the first English club to lift the trophy, fulfilling what had become an obsession after the tragedy of Munich 10 years earlier.

For England, Charlton made a similar, history-defining impact. A mainstay of the national side for over a decade, he played in four World Cups, and was integral to the success of the 1966 team, scoring three goals including two in the semi-final against Portugal. He was named European Footballer of the Year that same season.

In the 1970 tournament, age had caught up with him as he laboured in the withering heat of the semi-final against West Germany, but to this day, many still feel it was his substitution that cost England the victory. His 49 goals for England remains a record.

After such remarkable success with club and country, what came after was almost bound to be a letdown. Charlton finally called it a day at Old Trafford after 758 games, moving on to an unsuccessful spell as Preston manager and then player-manager.

He wasn't the first – and will certainly not be the last – great player to find the transition to management difficult, but in his directorial and ambassadorial roles for United, and as a football knight of the realm, his standing in the game is unsurpassed.

Charlton's mother Cissie playing football with him and his brothers Gordon and Tommy. The story that she was effectively his coach and football mentor has been overstated over the years. She was naturally delighted and relieved to welcome him home to Ashington from Munich in February 1958.

The brothers Charlton. Bobby and Jack have not always enjoyed a good relationship, but were both key members of the victorious 1966 England World Cup side.

" *Some people tell me that we professional players are soccer slaves. Well, if this is slavery, give me a life sentence.*

Bobby Charlton "

LEFT: All smiles at Preston North End in July 1973, but Charlton found management a struggle and, amid talk of disputes with the board over transfer activity, he resigned two years later.

RIGHT: Thirty-six years later, Bobby and the then surviving boys of '66 gather together once more.

DANNY BLANCHFLOWER

Danny Blanchflower combined intelligence on and off the field to establish himself as one of the most gifted footballers of his generation, and a major reason for the success of one of the great postwar club sides.

> "You cannot lead from the middle of a pack."
>
> Danny Blanchflower

Midfield general: Danny Blanchflower dictated games from the heart of the pitch, as a calm, poised and wonderfully creative footballer.

Danny Blanchflower was a one-off. Few of his contemporaries could match his supreme skill on the pitch, but it was away from the action that he stood out as a unique individual. He was a highly intelligent man who could analyse, interpret and articulate the game (and much else besides) better than almost anyone. He also did it with a wit and personality that could infuriate some but made him hugely popular with many more.

Fundamental to Blanchflower's character was his spirit of independent thinking that challenged stuffy convention. His career straddled two eras: the traditional days of the 1950s when footballers were supposed to know their place and keep quiet, and the more liberated 1960s when players could better assert and express themselves. None would do so more eloquently than Blanchflower, nor put it to such innovative use in the context of a football team.

His father was a craftsman in the Belfast shipyards and his mother a spirited woman who had been no mean player herself in a local ladies' team. Their influence was clearly evident in their eldest child's attitude towards the sport he excelled in at an early age, and his healthy disrespect of undeserving authority.

Making the switch to England from Glentoran to Barnsley in 1949, Blanchflower swiftly excelled and made a further step up in class by joining Aston Villa two years later. However, while his game developed, success was elusive. His willingness to have his say on anything from tactics to how the sport was run rankled with the board. By 1954 Blanchflower was 28: at his peak but also at a crossroads. If he was to realize his ambitions, his next move had to be to the right club.

He went to Tottenham, and it proved to be a near-perfect match. Spurs were still run on resolutely traditional lines by their owners, but the club had a reputation for forward-thinking football that suited Blanchflower's philosophy. Managerial upheavals and an ageing team in decline, however, meant Blanchflower's early years at White Hart Lane were a struggle. Indeed at one point he looked set to leave as new manager Bill Nicholson dropped him from the side when Blanchflower was 33. This was an age at which many players were making their retirement plans, but both skipper and boss had other ideas. Blanchflower was brought

> " I consider this programme to be an invasion of privacy. Nobody is going to press-gang me into anything. "
>
> Danny Blanchflower, on refusing to appear as the subject of *This Is Your Life*

As they home in on the League title, Blanchflower leads the Spurs side out at his former club Aston Villa, March 1961. This was a month after he had famously turned down an appearance on TV show *This Is Your Life*.

back into Nicholson's developing side and within two years "Super Spurs" pulled off what had seemed an impossibility – winning a League and FA Cup double.

The pair were an unlikely couple: Nicholson the outwardly dour Yorkshireman, Blanchflower the garrulous Ulsterman. But they shared a football idealism that worked brilliantly, with the player putting into practice on the pitch what the manager devised off it.

Blanchflower could certainly talk a good game but he could also play it. He was world class, dictating a match with his control, passing and perception. He was a brilliant captain – not just a figurehead but a genuine leader, encouraging, directing and inspiring his team-mates.

Age and injury caught up with him and retirement came in 1964. He was not finished yet, however. The man who was twice Footballer of the Year focused on a journalistic career he had already been pursuing part-time, and brought his wisdom, charisma and sense of mischief to the printed and spoken word. It seemed he would be a natural for management but, passed over for the Spurs job when Nicholson stood down, he had only brief spells at Chelsea and as Northern Ireland manager. He died in 1993 after suffering from Alzheimer's, an ironically cruel end for a man of such obvious intellect and sharpness of thought.

RIGHT: Blanchflower introducing his team-mates to the Duke of Edinburgh before the 1962 FA Cup final in which Spurs defeated Burnley 3-1. Blanchflower was asked by the Duchess of Kent at the previous final why opponents Leicester City had their names on the backs of their tracksuits, but Spurs didn't. "Ah well, ma'am," he replied, "you see we all know each other."

Club	Appearances	Goals
Glentoran	124	7
Barnsley	68	2
Aston Villa	155	10
Tottenham Hotspur	382	21

Country	Appearances	Goals
Northern Ireland	56	2
TOTAL	**785**	**42**

Honours

League Title	1 (1960–61)
FA Cup	2 (1960–61, 1961–62)
European Cup Winners' Cup	1 (1962–63)

FOOTBALL –STATS–

Danny Blanchflower

Name: Robert Dennis Blanchflower
Born: Belfast, 10th February 1926
Died: 9th December 1993
Position: Right-half
Playing career: 1946–64

Blanchflower with his famous "Super Spurs".

LEFT: Blanchflower had been a key player in the successful Northern Ireland side that reached the quarter-finals of the World Cup in 1958. He is seen here appearing in a celebrity golf tournament in Bangor, County Down, 1981.

BELOW: Blanchflower and manager Bill Nicholson parading the FA Cup to huge acclaim in Tottenham in 1962. The pair did not always get on – Nicholson would often be exasperated by some of his skipper's actions and comments – but they were a hugely effective duo.

DENIS LAW

Nicknamed "The King", Law was a key part of the Old Trafford attacking triumvirate that swaggered through the English and European game, and was mercurial up front for his country.

> " *Denis Law was my idol. To me, he epitomises what it is to be a Scot; he had style, he had skill, he had that something extra which meant that when Denis was on the pitch, you couldn't take your eyes off him.*
>
> Sir Alex Ferguson
> "

> *The quickest-thinking player I ever saw.*
>
> Matt Busby

The Lawman delivers. With his familiar and much-imitated goal celebration, Denis Law takes the acclaim of the Old Trafford crowd after scoring the winner against Liverpool in December 1968.

When **FOOTBALL** *Was* **FOOTBALL**

As one of the greatest and most prolific strikers for one of the world's greatest clubs, and as a free-scoring international adored by the fans of his home nation, Denis Law rightly ranks as a true legend of the sport. It is for those goals – all 333 of them – that he is best known. But he was a terrific all-round player with a multitude of skills and talents, and a likeable and ebullient character whose humour, enthusiasm and passion for football was evident.

Law was born into a large and poor family in Aberdeen. He would have been expected to have been picked up either by his local side or one of the Glasgow giants. Instead he was scouted by and signed for Huddersfield Town – a club that had fallen a long way from its prewar heyday but one that retained some cachet in Division Two.

He proved so successful at Leeds Road that other bigger clubs came calling to compete for his services. Manchester City got him first for a record British fee but just a year later Torino lured him to Italy. Law played well but pined for a return to Britain. This time he was wooed by Matt Busby, the manager who had given Law his Scotland debut when Busby was in temporary charge of the national side, and so Law headed to the red half of Manchester for another record-setting fee of £115,000.

Clubs were prepared to spend big money on Law because he could reliably deliver the precious commodity of goals. As Busby's second great United team developed, Law came to the fore. In conjunction with George Best and Bobby Charlton, Law plundered English and European defences, racking up the goals and earning trophy honours. To his bitter disappointment he was injured for the 1968 European Cup final, but he had done much to lay the foundations for the triumph.

In the meantime he was setting records for Scotland, scoring 30 goals in just 55 games (a figure equalled by Kenny Dalglish but in twice the number of games), and becoming the only Scot to be hailed as European Footballer of the Year – an honour which was bestowed on him in 1964. At the age of 34 and having stopped playing club football, he was still good enough to have been taken to the 1974 tournament.

He had retired from the club game, that is, due in part to an extraordinary end to his career. As United struggled

Signing for United and a record fee of £115,000, overseen by manager Matt Busby and Gigi Peronace, one of the game's earliest agents, who brokered several deals between Italian and British clubs.

> " I have seldom felt so depressed as I did that weekend.
>
> **Denis Law on scoring that goal for Manchester City against Manchester United** "

to cope with Busby's own retirement, Law was moved on to rivals Manchester City. It tore at Law's loyalties, but he was professional to the end, scoring an impudent back-heeled goal at Old Trafford as United went down into Division Two. It was not, contrary to common belief, the goal that decided United's fate, but Law reacted as if it might as well have been, and pointedly refused to celebrate.

When he hung his boots up for good, Law became an informed and entertaining pundit and undertook extensive charity work. While he played for both Manchester sides, it is at United that he is commemorated in a statue and still rightly known as "The King".

ABOVE: Law's upbringing was loving but tough – he reportedly did not wear shoes until he was 12. Seen here at the Aberdeen junior trials, he was tiny and wore glasses.

RIGHT: Sharing a light-hearted moment with a photographer during a 1965 game against Birmingham City.

Club	Appearances	Goals
Huddersfield Town	91	19
Manchester City	79	37
Torino	28	10
Manchester United	404	237
Country	**Appearances**	**Goals**
Scotland	55	30
TOTAL	**657**	**333**

Honours

League Title	2 (1964–65, 1966–67)
FA Cup	1 (1963)

FOOTBALL
–STATS–
Denis Law

Name: Denis Law
Born: Aberdeen, 24th February 1940
Position: Centre-forward
Playing career: 1956–74

> "Up there with the all-time greats. Electric. As a bloke and as a pal he's different class."
>
> George Best

Few Scotsmen have worn the dark blue shirt with such pride and success as Law. He is congratulated by team-mates Willie Henderson and Pat Crerand on scoring to secure a 2-2 draw in the Home International in April 1965. He would also star in the famous 3-2 win for the Scots over the reigning World Cup holders in 1967.

ABOVE: Probably as a legacy of his scrawny build as a child and his determination to prove doubters wrong, Law was a very feisty competitor. He had numerous run-ins with referees and opponents, and was not afraid to square up to anyone – including Jack Charlton in 1965.

BELOW: Opening his shoe repair shop in Blackley, Manchester, March 1964.

JIMMY GREAVES

While his haul of silverware did not quite match his penalty-area prowess, Jimmy Greaves still ranks as English football's most prolific top-level player, and one who defined the art of goalscoring.

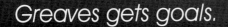

> *Greaves gets goals.*
>
> Dave Mackay

A spring in his step. Jimmy Greaves, goalscorer extraordinaire, rises high in a 5-0 FA Cup replay for Spurs against Bradford City in 1970.

Jimmy Greaves did not win many trophies – only a couple of FA Cups and one European honour in a 14-year career. He missed out on English football's greatest day, initially owing to injury but then a decision to drop him. On that day in 1966 Greaves was dressed in a suit rather than a red Three Lions shirt as his compatriots danced around the Wembley turf celebrating victory in the World Cup final. But if there is an element of underachievement about Greaves' career, he still is regarded by many in the know as the greatest English striker of all time – bar none.

His record speaks for itself. He scored the most goals ever in England's top flight and had six seasons as the First Division's leading goalscorer. He also broke various club and international records and is still the national side's third-highest goalscorer, despite earning fewer caps than many who played in his position.

But Greaves didn't just score goals and plenty of them. He executed them with elegance, precision, power and unerring accuracy, drawing on his flawless technique. In truth he didn't do much else, but in the simple words of his manager at Spurs, Bill Nicholson, "Jimmy didn't just blast the ball into the net – he passed it." If goalscoring is an art, then Greaves was its supreme master.

Raised in the borderlands of East London and Essex, Greaves was a youthful prodigy on the radar of a number of clubs, but it was Chelsea who secured the 15-year-old's signature and he became another of "Drakes Ducklings". He scored on his full debut in 1957 – a recurring theme of his career – and soon became the most talked-about and coveted young forward in the country. Despite Chelsea's indifferent form, Greaves was the model of consistency, racing to 100 career goals by the time he was just 20, the youngest player ever to do so.

Such eye-catching talent had various clubs clamouring for his transfer and Greaves was given a move to Italy and AC Milan in 1961. The high wages and lifestyle were little compensation, however. He loathed the dictatorial management style of Nereo Rocco and yearned for a return home. This came with a switch to his boyhood favourites Spurs in December 1961 for the sum of £99,999 – the figure famously set by Nicholson so as not to burden Greaves with the tag of being the first £100,000 player.

LEFT: Photographed for posterity as Greaves plays his final game for Chelsea. He scored all four goals in a 4-3 win over Nottingham Forest.

BELOW: Ciao Milano – Arrivederci Italia. Greaves' stay in Italy was a short one. Unable to settle, he lasted just four months before a return to England and Division One.

"
It's a funny old game.

Jimmy Greaves
"

FOOTBALL –STATS–

Jimmy Greaves

Club	Appearances	Goals
Chelsea	169	132
AC Milan	14	9
Tottenham Hotspur	380	266
West Ham United	40	13

Country	Appearances	Goals
England	57	44
TOTAL	**660**	**464**

Honours

FA Cup	2 (1962, 1967)
European Cup Winners' Cup	1 (1963)
World Cup	1* (1966)

* Greaves and the rest of the England squad who did not play in the final received winner's medals in 2009

Name: James Peter Greaves
Born: East Ham, 20th February 1940
Position: Centre-forward
Playing career: 1957–71

The marriage between Greaves and Tottenham would prove to be a joyous one. While it did not reap the League titles that might have been expected by uniting the country's then best team with the nation's best goalscorer, it resulted in outstanding and hugely entertaining football. Greaves scored a hat-trick on his Spurs debut, scored in his first FA Cup final appearance and scored twice in the European Cup Winners' Cup final in 1963. He scored from close range, rattled in hat-tricks from all angles and went on mazy, goalscoring runs that left team-mates, opponents and frenzied crowds gasping in astonishment. Two in particular stand out: an oft-replayed goal against Manchester United in 1965 and an even better one against Leicester City in 1968.

No cameras were present to record that beauty and so Spurs fans who were there can tell ever taller tales of how great a goal it was. In truth it needed little embellishment. It simply provided emphatic illustration of the genius of a player who ended up as Tottenham's greatest ever goalscorer.

Matters were less happy with England. While Greaves had played in the 1962 World Cup, the 1966 finals promised to be *his* tournament. It was not to be. Injury and then the decision of manager Alf Ramsey to opt for the teamwork capabilities of Geoff Hurst rather than the maverick talent of Greaves forced his exclusion. The choice was vindicated, but missing out on the final would haunt Greaves for years. By 1970, drink was starting to take its toll. He was sold by Spurs for a brief spell at West Ham, before alcohol took a firm grip.

Few sporting declines have been laid as bare as Greaves'. The title of his autobiography was *This One's On Me*. It alluded to his severe drink problem but also his honesty in first confronting and then recovering from his personal demons. He went on to forge a highly successful media career, where his forthright, outspoken but often humorous views on football and the wider world earned him widespread popularity. Greaves talked the game like he played it – incisive and straight to the point, but invariably with a smile on his face.

ABOVE: Greaves thrived back in London with Spurs.

Being mobbed by autograph hunters after training in 1967, shortly before Greaves won his second FA Cup winner's medal. Greaves was adored at Spurs. In a decade when the club enjoyed its true glory days, and a succession of great players graced White Hart Lane, Greaves holds his own and is still ranked by many Spurs fans as their favourite player.

"
The boy is a natural.

Danny Blanchflower
"

Greaves emerged from the despair of alcoholism to carve out a new and successful career in television and media. His long-time association with 1960s contemporary Ian St John resulted in the highly successful football review show called *On the Ball* and later the popular Saturday lunchtime programme *Saint and Greavesie*. Here the pair rub shoulders with Liverpool comic Jimmy Tarbuck at the Variety Club Awards in February 1986.

BOBBY MOORE

The English footballing hero who will never grow old, Bobby Moore was taken tragically early in life, but his standing in the game is unmatched – and even grows with the passage of time.

"He was the spirit and the heartbeat of the team. A cool, calculating footballer I could trust with my life. He was the supreme professional, the best I ever worked with. Without him England would never have won the World Cup.

Sir Alf Ramsey

Her Majesty the Queen presents the Jules Rimet trophy to captain Bobby Moore on English football's most famous day, 30th July 1966.

> "We were more than a team. We were a formidable nation, bonded and held together by our will to win for England.

Bobby Moore

Is there a more evocative, inspiring and emotional image in English football than the sight of Bobby Moore parading the Jules Rimet trophy? The golden boy of the game, held aloft by his team-mates in the moment of victory and celebrating England's finest hour. It is the pinnacle of achievement that schoolboy dreams are made of and Moore not only realized the honour but lived up to it perfectly.

He was just 25 in 1966. A glittering career seemed to lie before him. That he did not go on to further glory as a player, nor achieve gilded success in management arguably says as much about the English game as it does Moore's limitations, but in truth, it was an impossible act to follow.

One of a steady stream of players reared in suburban East London in the postwar era, Moore was born amid the chaos of the Blitz but emerged as a young player with unnerving composure and maturity beyond his years. He signed for West Ham and flourished under the management of Ron Greenwood, winning FA Cup and European Cup Winners' Cup medals in successive seasons.

It was not all a bed of roses at Upton Park; ongoing disputes and snubs by the owners blocked moves away, notably to Spurs. But amid this behind-the-scenes discord, Moore was the model of dependability and excellence. A born leader who inspired by example rather than relying on crude force or shouting, he was an idol even to his team-mates. As a defender he was supreme. This was never better illustrated than in the dying moments of the 1966 World Cup final. With England desperate to run down the clock, Moore gained possession. Rather than hoof the ball as far away as possible, he lofted a simple but assured ball to Geoff Hurst. The rest – with people on the pitch thinking it was all over – is unforgettable, tear-jerking history.

Before Moore accepted the trophy from the Queen, he famously wiped his hands, not wanting to besmirch the monarch's pristine white gloves. It revealed much about the man. He was immaculate in his football and equally elegant away from it. As a good-looking lad tailor-made for the 1960s he was one of a new breed of working-class young men made good. Advertisers

RIGHT: Proudly presenting West Ham's 1964 trophy haul – the FA Cup and the Charity Shield.

BELOW: Moore was the star pupil of the famous West Ham academy.

Club	Appearances	Goals
West Ham United	646	27
Fulham	150	1
Country	**Appearances**	**Goals**
England	108	2
TOTAL	**904**	**30**

Honours

FA Cup	1 (1964)
European Cup Winners' Cup	1 (1965)
World Cup	1 (1966)

FOOTBALL -STATS-

Bobby Moore

Name: Robert Frederick Chelsea Moore

Born: Barking, 12th April 1941

Died: 24th February 1993

Position: Centre-half

Playing career: 1958–77

RIGHT: Moore in action with his great friend Jimmy Greaves. Moore lacked pace and was not the most powerful of defenders, but his technique was immaculate, he timed tackles to perfection and his reading of the game was unmatched.

simply adored his effortless cool and used him to front a number of campaigns.

For all that, Moore was not quite the unblemished saint of popular image. He liked a drink and could more than hold his own among some of the most prolific boozers of the game. He made mistakes both on and off the field. But if these are flaws, they are understandable ones and only add to his appeal as a rounded human being who achieved remarkable things.

After 1966 he continued to lead club and country and made headlines in the World Cup of 1970; firstly after being caught up in a bizarre accusation of shoplifting in a hotel jewellery store in Colombia, and then as captain of arguably England's greatest ever side. They fell at the quarter-final stage as West Germany exacted revenge for defeat four years earlier, but the tournament offered a number of memorable moments, not least Moore's outstanding tackle on Pelé in the classic against Brazil.

Thereafter Moore's career was one of acclaim, but also frustration. He moved to Fulham for a mid-1970s swansong, before leading the soccer revolution in North America. He failed in management at Oxford City and Southend, but his media career as a laconic and expert pundit showed he had lost none of his appreciation for the finer points of the game. Colon cancer robbed him and his family of his elder years, but with typical modesty he kept his condition quiet until the near end. He died aged just 51. A nation mourned but also cherished and said a heartfelt thanks for the memories.

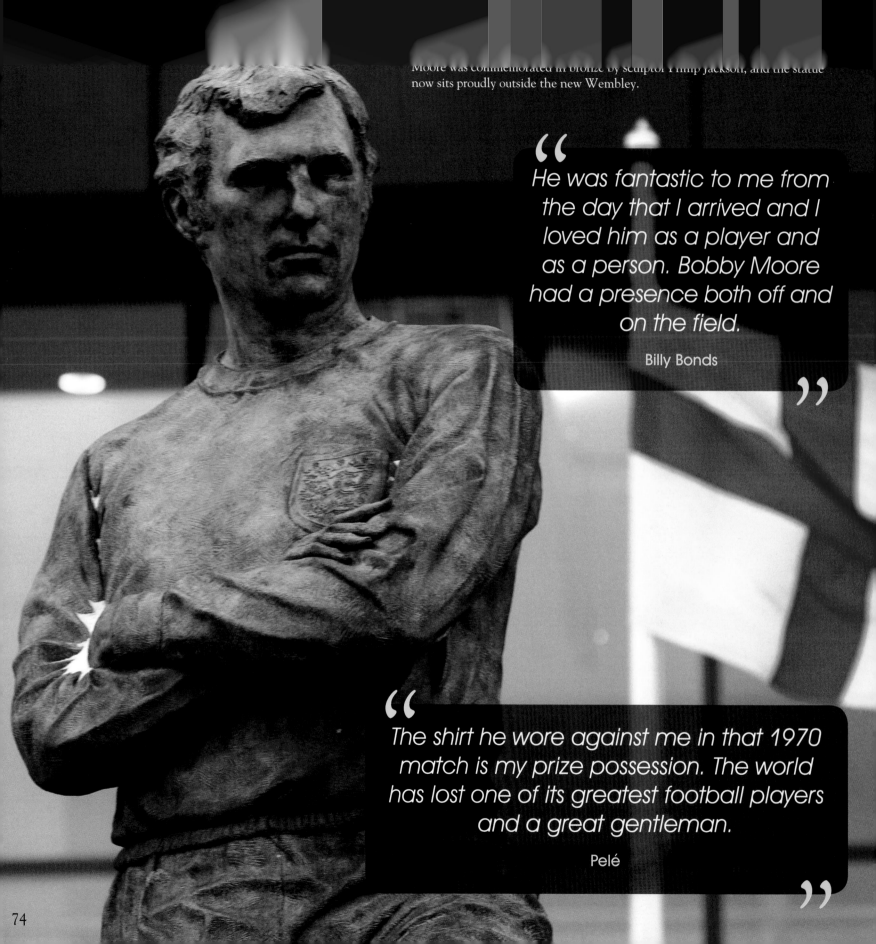

> " He was fantastic to me from the day that I arrived and I loved him as a player and as a person. Bobby Moore had a presence both off and on the field. "
>
> Billy Bonds

> " The shirt he wore against me in that 1970 match is my prize possession. The world has lost one of its greatest football players and a great gentleman. "
>
> Pelé

RIGHT: Playing for laughs. Moore was a hugely popular friend and colleague, with a fine sense of humour.

BELOW: Ten days before his retirement from English football, Moore was in reflective mood sitting in the Craven Cottage dressing room with his famous number 6 shirt hanging on its peg.

DAVE MACKAY

Mackay was not just an outstanding player but a footballing force of nature whose extraordinary will to win drove his sides to success. He is also one of that select band to have won League titles as a player and manager.

> " *The hardest man I have ever played against.*
>
> George Best "

The irrepressible Dave Mackay returns from a double leg break to leap over team-mates Cliff Jones, Ron Henry and Jimmy Greaves.

When FOOTBALL *Was* FOOTBALL

77

There are many things to admire about the modern game, but there is one aspect that many older fans often say they miss. These supporters pine for the days when the tough guys of the sport would put their bodies on the line for the cause of their team. The hard man has become almost non-existent.

Few lived up to the label more fittingly than Dave Mackay – but crucially, he was also fair. He was a force of nature committed to the pursuit of winning football matches, and would let no one stand in his way. But he didn't cheat, bully or deliberately harm to achieve his objectives. As if that wasn't enough, he was also some player.

Mackay made his name with his home-town club Hearts. He had been the standout player at Tynecastle, adored by the home crowd who were thrilled by his determination and dynamism. Such talent inevitably attracted the attentions of clubs south of the border. Despite the protests of Hearts fans desperate to keep their unique talent, Mackay headed to England, and moved to Spurs in 1959 for £32,000.

Seen as a big sum in those days, it would prove to be one of the great bargain buys. Mackay was the all-action midfield general who breathed fire into the emerging Spurs team and drove them on to the Double and memorable European campaigns. On the training pitch and in the gym he had to win every challenge, every drill and every small-sided game he played in. Out on the pitch for real he tackled with an almost unprecedented intensity, passed with refinement and purpose, launched incisive attacks and chipped in with crucial goals.

His energy and physicality justifiably put fear into opponents but it was his all-round ability that made him a truly great player. Mackay loathed the hardman image, in part because it overshadowed what a fine and highly skilled player he was, and also how fundamental he was to Tottenham's thrilling style of play.

That became even more evident with his absence. Alongside the retirement of Danny Blanchflower and the tragic death of John White, Mackay's protracted lay-offs due to a double leg break effectively meant

You don't fancy this, do you?

Dave Mackay to the Chelsea players in the tunnel before the 1967 FA Cup final (Spurs won 2-1)

FOOTBALL
–STATS–
Dave Mackay

Name: David Craig Mackay

Born: Musselburgh, 14th November 1934

Position: Half-back

Playing career: 1953–72

Club	Appearances	Goals
Hearts	208	32
Tottenham Hotspur	318	51
Derby County	145	5
Swindon Town	26	1

Country	Appearances	Goals
Scotland	22	4
TOTAL	**719**	**93**

Honours

League Title	1 (1960–61)
FA Cup	3 (1961, 1962, 1967)
As a manager	1 League title (1974–75)

the end for the Double side. Yet with typical bravery he battled back to win further honours, leaving Spurs as a bona fide hero in 1968.

If anyone thought Mackay was in decline, however, he had other ideas. Derby County manager Brian Clough realized the Scotsman still had much to offer and he was instrumental in the East Midlanders winning promotion in 1968–69. A playing swansong at Swindon was followed by managerial spells at the County Ground and then Nottingham Forest. When Clough and Peter Taylor clashed with the Derby board and left the Baseball Ground, Mackay stepped in and managed Derby to another League Championship in 1974–75. There were additional jobs in the Middle East, as well as mixed records at Walsall, Doncaster Rovers and Birmingham City.

Underutilized by his country, Mackay never played as many internationals as his talent merited – there was a lingering suspicion that those players who had left Scotland for England were deliberately sidelined – but the national side's loss was club football's gain. Whether on the field or in the dugout, Dave Mackay was a true inspiration. He may have only been 5ft 7in, but he was a colossus.

LEFT: Mackay was a hero at Hearts and fans demonstrated against his move to Spurs in 1959.

RIGHT: On all-too-rare international duty.

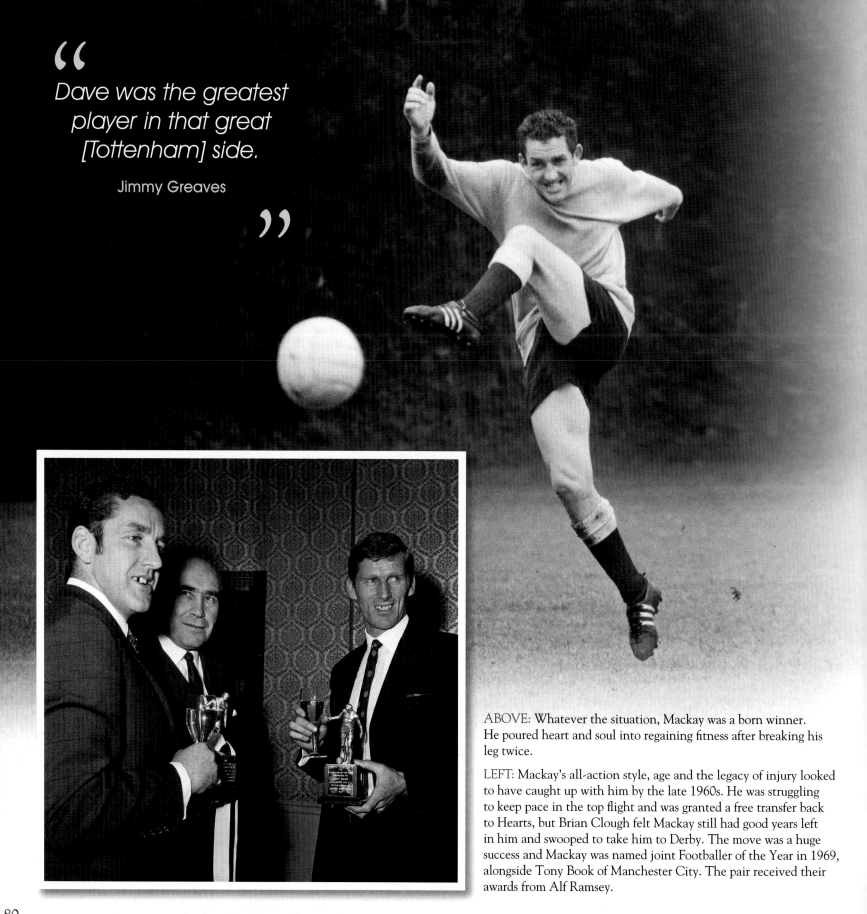

> *Dave was the greatest player in that great [Tottenham] side.*
>
> Jimmy Greaves

ABOVE: Whatever the situation, Mackay was a born winner. He poured heart and soul into regaining fitness after breaking his leg twice.

LEFT: Mackay's all-action style, age and the legacy of injury looked to have caught up with him by the late 1960s. He was struggling to keep pace in the top flight and was granted a free transfer back to Hearts, but Brian Clough felt Mackay still had good years left in him and swooped to take him to Derby. The move was a huge success and Mackay was named joint Footballer of the Year in 1969, alongside Tony Book of Manchester City. The pair received their awards from Alf Ramsey.

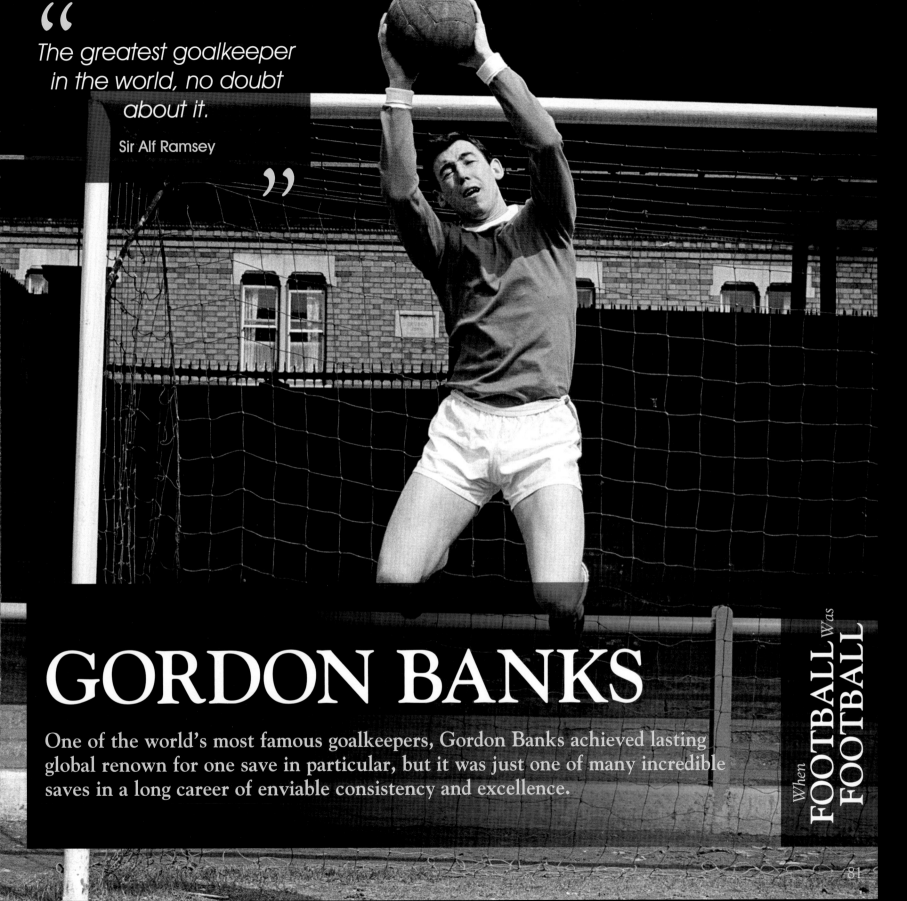

> "The greatest goalkeeper in the world, no doubt about it."
>
> Sir Alf Ramsey

GORDON BANKS

One of the world's most famous goalkeepers, Gordon Banks achieved lasting global renown for one save in particular, but it was just one of many incredible saves in a long career of enviable consistency and excellence.

When FOOTBALL *Was* FOOTBALL

Footballers – especially the modern ones – will always have their detractors. It takes a special kind of player to be universally loved and admired. Gordon Banks did not play for particularly star-studded or successful clubs, which might partly explain his universal popularity, but in any case his talent and character alone will always ensure he has a special place in the hearts of all genuine football fans.

As one of the heroes of 1966, he will be forever identified with England's World Cup-winning side. He was in fact a fixture for the national team for over a decade. His finest individual moment came in the 1970 tournament when he somehow turned away Pelé's bullet-like downward header, springing low and to his right to palm the ball away. A telling illustration of the sheer brilliance and memorable nature of the save came during the 2014 World Cup, when a great stop by the Mexican keeper Ochoa denied Brazil – Banks trended on Twitter in the immediate aftermath, as fans rushed to make a comparison with the better stop made nearly 50 years earlier.

Banks' overall career ranged over three very different decades. He was born in South Yorkshire but began his professional journey in the 1950s further south with Chesterfield, before Leicester City provided him with the opportunity to step up to Division One. Twice he was an FA Cup runner-up, but his high level of performance led to an England call-up, where his dependability and all-round capabilities provided the national side with its foundation.

Banks played in 23 consecutive England matches from 1964, and in 73 overall appearances kept 35 clean sheets. He was a brilliant shot-stopper, commanding his area, and a resolute last line of defence his team-mates could always count on.

Banks' agility was positively gymnastic. It didn't just come naturally, but was honed in endless hours of training and practice. Coupled with lightning-fast reflexes, it made Banks the pre-eminent goalkeeper of the era. That, remarkably, wasn't enough to save him from the chop at his club. Leicester had a young Peter Shilton coming through the ranks and, amid considerable rancour, sold the older man to Stoke City. A move to Liverpool, Leeds or one of the other big clubs at the time would have enabled Banks to win major honours, but his time in the Potteries was enjoyable and he continued his brilliant form.

Mexico 1970 showed how much he was worth to England – not just for his performances but for how much his absence hurt the team. When he was taken ill with a stomach upset before the quarter-final against West Germany, Alf Ramsey cursed his luck. There were mutterings of plots and deliberate food poisoning, but to little avail. Without "Banks of England", the Three Lions lost.

Banks cuts a solitary figure as his Leicester side go in search of an equalizer against Wolves in 1960.

> "At that moment I hated Gordon Banks . . . but [it was] the greatest save I had ever seen."
>
> Pelé on Banks' save in 1970

With his career winding down, Banks had a few more spectacular performances left in him, notably an epic extra-time penalty showdown with England colleague Geoff Hurst in a 1972 League Cup semi-final. Banks came out on top. His career was effectively ended, however, the moment he was seriously injured in a car crash in 1972, losing the sight in his right eye.

He attempted a comeback of sorts in North America but, hampered by his loss of vision, it was in vain. There were unsuccessful attempts at a managerial career and mixed fortunes in business – but in retirement Banks remained an immensely popular figure.

BELOW RIGHT: Honours were in relatively short supply for such a world-class player but Banks' joy was clear in victory for Stoke over Chelsea in the 1972 League Cup final.

BELOW: On the eve of the 1972 League Cup final, bouquets for Banks – himself, according to the caption of the day, "an ardent rose grower".

Club	Appearances	Goals
Chesterfield	26	0
Leicester City	356	0
Stoke City	250	0

Country	Appearances	Goals
England	73	0
TOTAL	**705**	**0**

Honours

League Cup	2 (1964, 1972)
World Cup	1 (1966)

FOOTBALL –STATS–

Gordon Banks

Name: Gordon Banks
Born: Sheffield, 30th December 1937
Position: Goalkeeper
Playing career: 1955–72

"Banks of England" in action during
the World Cup final of 1966.

> " . . . *every goal is like a*
> *knife in the ribs.*
>
> Gordon Banks "

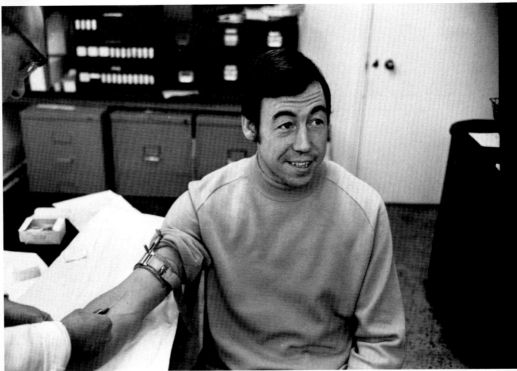

ABOVE: As part of England's build-up for the 1970 Mexico World Cup, Banks and the rest of the players visited St Mary's Hospital for blood tests.

BELOW: Footballers and golf? It'll never catch on . . .

MARTIN PETERS

An elegant and composed footballer, Martin Peters was the youthful star of the 1966 World Cup and a club favourite at West Ham, Spurs and Norwich.

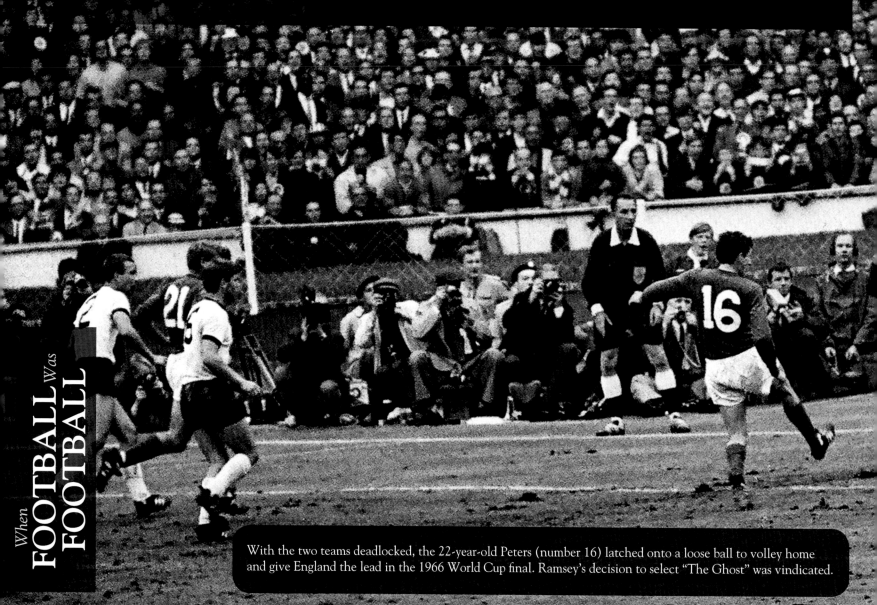

With the two teams deadlocked, the 22-year-old Peters (number 16) latched onto a loose ball to volley home and give England the lead in the 1966 World Cup final. Ramsey's decision to select "The Ghost" was vindicated.

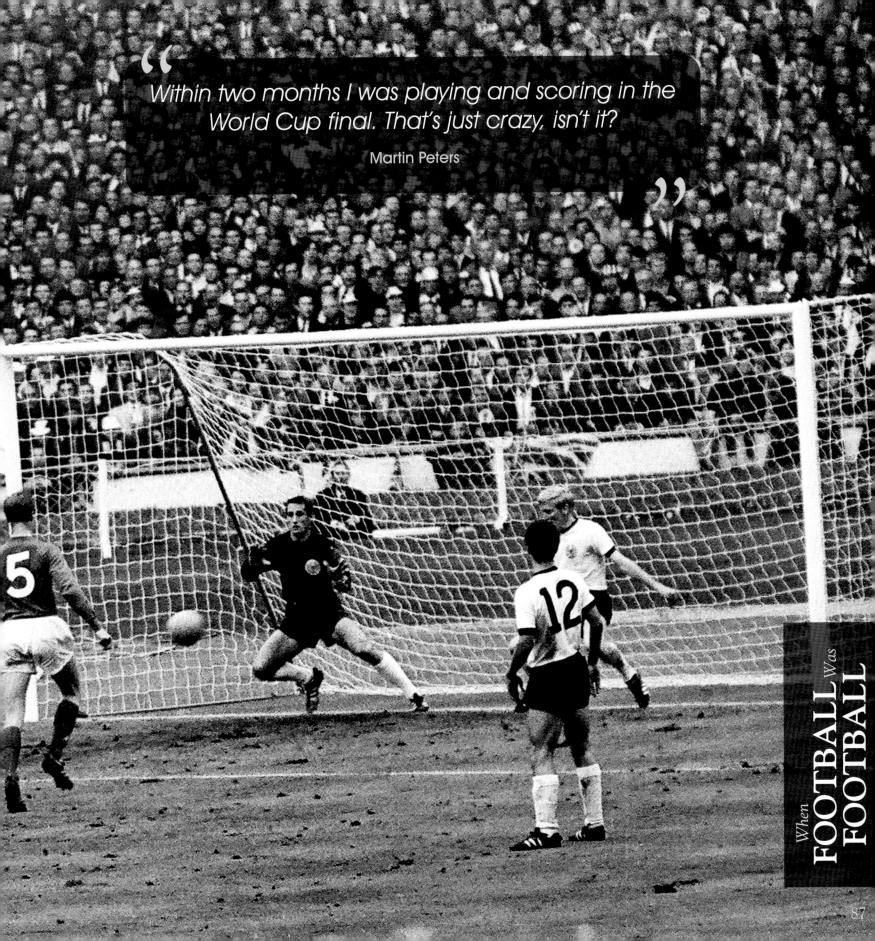

> *"Within two months I was playing and scoring in the World Cup final. That's just crazy, isn't it?"*
>
> Martin Peters

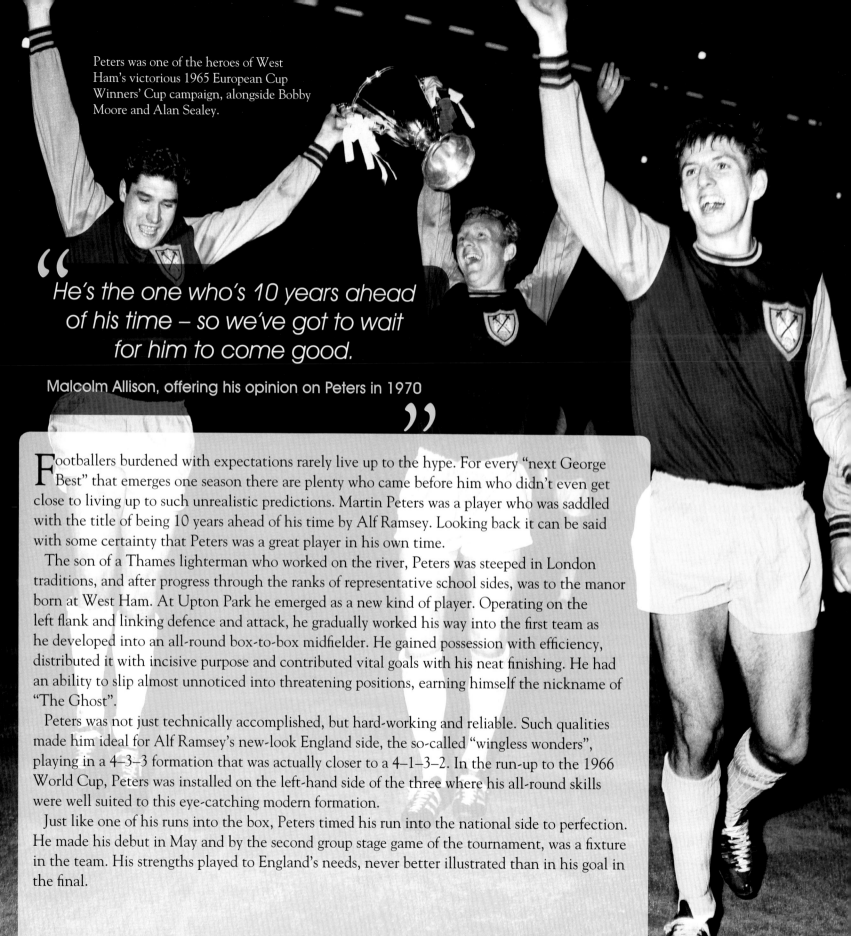

Peters was one of the heroes of West Ham's victorious 1965 European Cup Winners' Cup campaign, alongside Bobby Moore and Alan Sealey.

> " *He's the one who's 10 years ahead of his time – so we've got to wait for him to come good.* "

Malcolm Allison, offering his opinion on Peters in 1970

Footballers burdened with expectations rarely live up to the hype. For every "next George Best" that emerges one season there are plenty who came before him who didn't even get close to living up to such unrealistic predictions. Martin Peters was a player who was saddled with the title of being 10 years ahead of his time by Alf Ramsey. Looking back it can be said with some certainty that Peters was a great player in his own time.

The son of a Thames lighterman who worked on the river, Peters was steeped in London traditions, and after progress through the ranks of representative school sides, was to the manor born at West Ham. At Upton Park he emerged as a new kind of player. Operating on the left flank and linking defence and attack, he gradually worked his way into the first team as he developed into an all-round box-to-box midfielder. He gained possession with efficiency, distributed it with incisive purpose and contributed vital goals with his neat finishing. He had an ability to slip almost unnoticed into threatening positions, earning himself the nickname of "The Ghost".

Peters was not just technically accomplished, but hard-working and reliable. Such qualities made him ideal for Alf Ramsey's new-look England side, the so-called "wingless wonders", playing in a 4–3–3 formation that was actually closer to a 4–1–3–2. In the run-up to the 1966 World Cup, Peters was installed on the left-hand side of the three where his all-round skills were well suited to this eye-catching modern formation.

Just like one of his runs into the box, Peters timed his run into the national side to perfection. He made his debut in May and by the second group stage game of the tournament, was a fixture in the team. His strengths played to England's needs, never better illustrated than in his goal in the final.

He was a World Cup winner with only eight caps and at the age of just 22. A gilded club career beckoned, but it appeared to stall at West Ham. Looking for a move, Peters drew the eye of Bill Nicholson, and was transferred in 1970 to Spurs for a record £200,000, with Jimmy Greaves the makeweight in the deal. At White Hart Lane Peters flourished, working tirelessly, spreading play and proving invaluable in attack. It led to further trophy success at home and in Europe, and established him not only as Tottenham captain but as one of the country's best.

He played with quiet efficiency rather than chest-thumping, conspicuous effort, which contributed to many Spurs fans only truly appreciating his value when he left, this time for Norwich City. Tottenham's hastily conceived loss was the Norfolk side's gain. Peters played over 200 more games and played a major part in the club establishing itself in the top flight.

A brief spell as player-manager at Sheffield United preceded retirement. Peters has since worked in insurance, as a non-executive director at Spurs and as matchday host at both White Hart Lane and Upton Park – a modest, understated man enduringly popular at both clubs.

Club	Appearances	Goals
West Ham United	364	100
Tottenham Hotspur	262	76
Norwich City	232	50
Sheffield United	24	3

Country	Appearances	Goals
England	67	20
TOTAL	**949**	**249**

Honours

European Cup Winners' Cup	1 (1965)
UEFA Cup	1 (1972)
League Cup	2 (1971, 1973)
World Cup	1 (1966)

FOOTBALL –STATS–

Martin Peters

Name: Martin Stanford Peters

Born: Plaistow, 8th November 1943

Position: Midfielder

Playing career: 1962–81

Peters, seen here alongside Pat Jennings, skippered Spurs to League Cup triumph in 1973.

Alan Mullery (centre) and Steve Perryman (right) welcome the new record signing to White Hart Lane in September 1970.

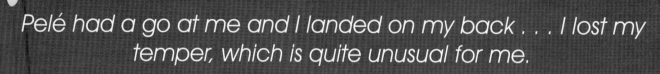

Pelé had a go at me and I landed on my back . . . I lost my temper, which is quite unusual for me.

Martin Peters

Lying back and thinking of England glory amid the frenzy of the World Cup, 10th July 1966.

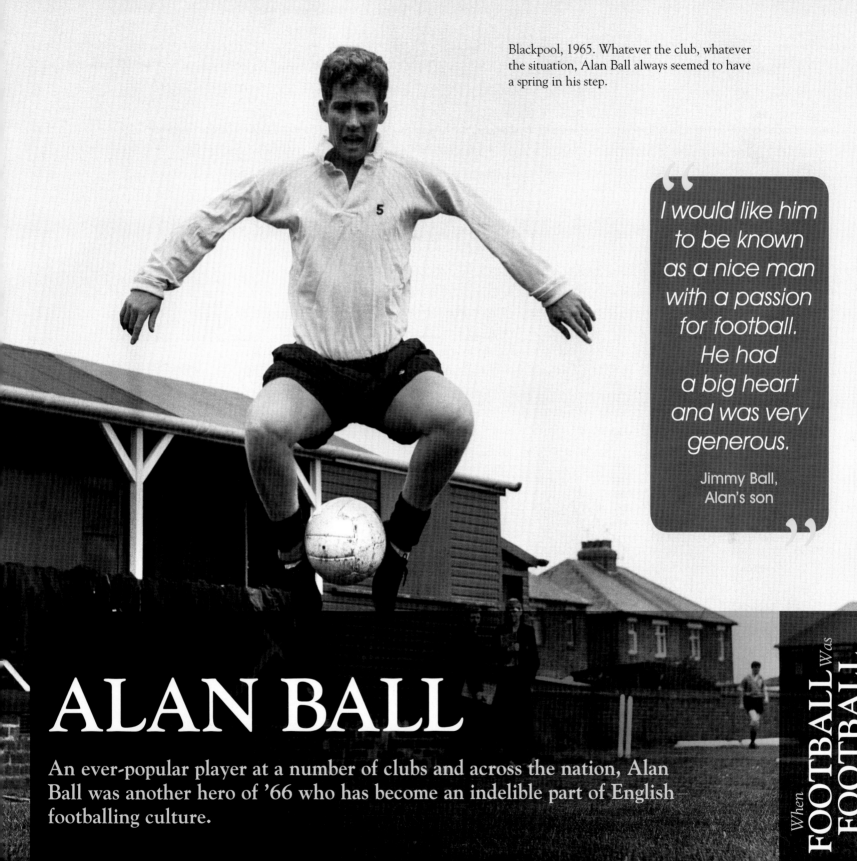

Blackpool, 1965. Whatever the club, whatever the situation, Alan Ball always seemed to have a spring in his step.

> *I would like him to be known as a nice man with a passion for football. He had a big heart and was very generous.*
>
> Jimmy Ball,
> Alan's son

ALAN BALL

An ever-popular player at a number of clubs and across the nation, Alan Ball was another hero of '66 who has become an indelible part of English footballing culture.

The mop of ginger hair, the squeaky voice and the effervescent approach to life and the game: Alan Ball's death at the age of just 61 robbed his family and the sport of one of its most cherished and distinctive sons. As a tenacious midfielder for club and country, he was a great player and as a character with seemingly boundless enthusiasm for the game he was charm itself.

An enthusiastic competitor, he invited the inevitable label of "midfield terrier". To some extent Ball almost defined that description, but that overshadows his broader talent. He was an accomplished all-round player with a fine touch, great vision and a keen eye for goal.

From the start of his career Ball was a born winner and a human dynamo. At just 5ft 6in he was disadvantaged in the English game that still prided physicality as much as skill, but he inherited from father Alan senior – who had played in the lower leagues – a determination to succeed and prove any doubters wrong. After initial rejection from a number of clubs, the 16-year-old Ball was taken on at Blackpool, who in those days were still a force in the game.

Improving season by season and contributing his fair share of goals, Ball showed the kind of all-round ability, stamina and drive that Alf Ramsey was looking for as he assembled a side to challenge for the World Cup. Ball made his debut for the Three Lions a year before the tournament but his place was not assured. It wasn't until the famously spiteful quarter-final against Argentina that his true worth to the team was shown. Ball, with his ceaseless industry and runs down the right flank (rather ironically for a team nicknamed the "wingless wonders"), was now instrumental in how the side functioned. In the eyes of many it wasn't Hurst who was man of the match in the final but Ball.

Amid the post-World Cup euphoria, Everton moved swiftly to sign Ball for £110,000, and he would go on to enjoy his best club years at Goodison. As part of manager Harry Catterick's famed "Holy Trinity", Ball – along with Howard Kendall and Colin Harvey – was instrumental in the Toffees winning the 1969–70 League title.

After five years on Merseyside, Ball was on the move again, this time to newly crowned Double winners Arsenal. There were no further trophies at Highbury but plenty more of Ball's familiar graft and guile in midfield. Another switch to the south coast and Southampton saw him enjoy a long and fruitful end to his career, though in a remarkable twist, it completed a hat-trick of moving to clubs just after they had won the FA Cup – though Ball was never to win it himself.

Instead, after brief spells at Bristol Rovers and North American clubs, Ball embarked on a decidedly varied managerial career. He managed no fewer than seven clubs but was best known for his two spells at Portsmouth (in the first of which he won promotion), some thrilling relegation escapes at Southampton, and a less celebrated but high-profile short spell in what was then the managers' graveyard of Manchester City.

Despite this mixed record, Ball remained a popular figure across the nation. It was a reflection of the universal affection his team-mates had for him. His nickname was "Bouncy", an apt description for his ceaseless energy, positive attitude and sunny disposition.

His death understandably hit family, his many friends and colleagues hard. He had gone too soon at 61. But it was a mark of Ball's immensely likeable and infectious nature that those remembering him would do so with a warm smile.

One last look around Goodison Park as Ball collects his boots and prepares to move on to pastures new.

Club	Appearances	Goals
Blackpool	164	49
Everton	254	80
Arsenal	218	52
Southampton	234	13
Bristol Rovers	17	2

Country	Appearances	Goals
England	72	8
TOTAL	**959**	**204**

Honours

League Title	1 (1969–70)
World Cup	1 (1966)

FOOTBALL
–STATS–

Alan Ball

Name: Alan James Ball

Born: Farnworth, 12th May 1945

Died: 25th April 2007

Position: Midfielder

Playing career: 1962–83

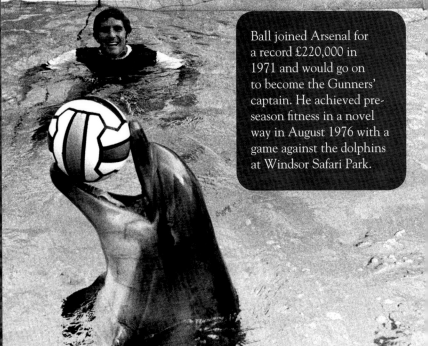

Ball joined Arsenal for a record £220,000 in 1971 and would go on to become the Gunners' captain. He achieved pre-season fitness in a novel way in August 1976 with a game against the dolphins at Windsor Safari Park.

Alan was a brave little fella. Everybody loved Alan; he was a lovely little lad.

Jack Charlton

Ball enjoyed a revival in his career at Southampton, helping the south coast side into Division One alongside fellow "Saints warriors" Peter Osgood, Ted MacDougall and Mick Channon. Behind them

> *Alan started life as a road sweeper and ended up as the best lead violinist Southampton ever had.*
>
> Lawrie McMenemy

Looking up to fellow World Cup winner and friend, Jack Charlton.

In the dugout at Southampton in 1994. Ball had a mixed time of it in management, but invariably kept smiling through. His trademark flat cap was placed on his coffin at his funeral in 2007.

GEOFF HURST

Forever identified with the 1966 World Cup final, Geoff Hurst's unique hat-trick has tended to overshadow the extent of his overall career and his all-round abilities.

> "As I was running towards the German goal, Alan Ball was shouting 'Hursty, Hursty, give me the ball!' I said to myself, 'Sod you, Bally, I'm on a hat trick.'"
>
> Geoff Hurst

Geoff Hurst – who says queueing is one of his pet hates – waits in line to have his medical checks prior to leaving for the Mexico World Cup in 1970.

In action for West Ham during the 1964 FA Cup final against Preston North End. Hurst scored the Hammers' second equalizer in a match they won 3-2.

"

The memories [of the World Cup final] are vivid, certainly of the game and a lot of the stuff surrounding it. I remember exactly what I did the next morning, which was cut the grass and wash my car.

Geoff Hurst

"

If ever a player seized his moment it was Geoff Hurst. In the run-up to the 1966 World Cup it seemed he would be playing understudy to the country's best and most prolific front man, Jimmy Greaves. An injury to Greaves after the game against France gave the younger man his chance, which he exploited with such vigour that he will forever be synonymous with World Cup glory.

For a man so readily identified with London and West Ham, Hurst's origins actually lie in Cheshire. His family moved to Essex when he was eight and there he became a fine talent in both football and cricket. The former eventually held sway (though he would turn out once for the Essex county team in 1962) and Hurst had a successful trial at West Ham.

Initially a left-half, Hurst was willing but not entirely able. It was manager Ron Greenwood's bold decision to convert Hurst into an out-and-out centre-forward that transformed the player's life. As a front man, Hurst swiftly prospered, racking up the goals in West Ham's magnificent march towards successive FA Cup and European Cup Winners' Cup triumphs.

Like his West Ham team-mates Bobby Moore and (more pertinently) Martin Peters, success with "The Academy" at Upton Park led to an England call-up. Alf Ramsey's interest had been sparked not only by Hurst's 40 goals in the 1965–66 season, but also his all-round play. Strong, fast and good in the air, Hurst was a player Ramsey saw as another valuable cog to fit into his England machine.

Both player and team clicked into gear at just the right time. Once installed in the front line he never looked back, scoring the winner against Argentina. In the final against West Germany, he had the kind of game dreams are made of – equalizing with a powerful header, before giving England the lead in extra-time with one of history's most memorable and controversial goals. As his shot crashed down from the crossbar, Hurst was adamant it had crossed the line and the Soviet linesman Tofik Bakhramov agreed – England were ahead again. The *coup de grâce* came in the final seconds as Hurst, showing the speed, stamina and composure that had so enthused Ramsey, smashed his third high into the net.

Anything else after that would be an anti-climax, but Hurst proved he was no flash in the pan with six more years of fine service with England and West Ham. He transferred to Stoke in 1972 before spells at West Brom and then in the USA. Like others among his 1966 contemporaries, a move into management was not successful. After being sacked by Chelsea in 1981, he focused on a successful business career in insurance, before retiring in 2002.

Sort of retiring, that is. Being a member of the only English side to win the World Cup and the only man to score a hat-trick in the final are honours Hurst will never be allowed to forget. After being knighted in 1998 he has spent much time patiently – and happily – sharing his memories and views on the game of which he has been such a star.

Club	Appearances	Goals
West Ham United	500	242
Stoke City	130	39
West Bromwich Albion	12	2

Country	Appearances	Goals
England	49	24
TOTAL	**691**	307

Honours

FA Cup	1 (1964)
European Cup Winners' Cup	1 (1965)
World Cup	1 (1966)

FOOTBALL −STATS−

Geoff Hurst

Name: Geoffrey Charles Hurst
Born: Ashton-under-Lyne, 8th December 1941
Position: Centre-forward
Playing career: 1959–76

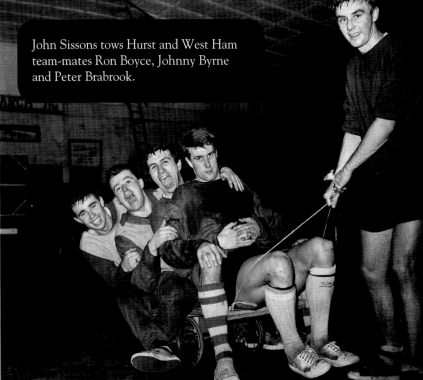

John Sissons tows Hurst and West Ham team-mates Ron Boyce, Johnny Byrne and Peter Brabrook.

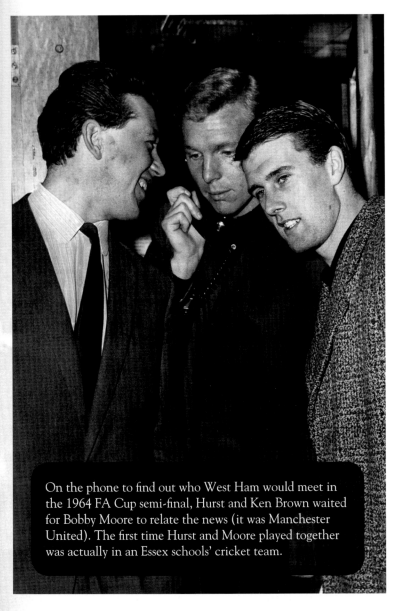

On the phone to find out who West Ham would meet in the 1964 FA Cup semi-final, Hurst and Ken Brown waited for Bobby Moore to relate the news (it was Manchester United). The first time Hurst and Moore played together was actually in an Essex schools' cricket team.

BELOW: Hurst holding his own in the familiar hustle and bustle of English football, this time for Stoke against Doncaster, 1972.

LEFT: Singing for England: Hurst was part of the line-up for the national side's 1970 World Cup song – and number one hit – 'Back Home'.

George Best, football immortal, takes the acclaim of an ecstatic Old Trafford crowd after a beautifully lobbed goal against Spurs in 1971.

> *"I was born with a great gift, and sometimes with that comes a destructive streak. Just as I wanted to outdo everyone when I played, I had to outdo everyone when we were out on the town.*
>
> George Best

GEORGE BEST

Icon, hero, superstar, playboy, flawed genius and a troubled man taken too soon. George Best was all these things and more, but primarily one of the game's greatest ever players.

So much has been said and written about George Best that it is sometimes difficult to separate fact from myth. Some things are more certain than others: he was a genuine world-class player. He was the first true "pop star" footballer, perfect for a new age in British sport and wider society. He was a naturally shy person who lived a high-profile, often hedonistic and ultimately short-lived existence. His ability and fame went way beyond merely excelling at his chosen trade. And George Best still captivates and enthrals us today as the complete, ultimate football legend.

His story has become part of the game's folklore. He was yet another player born into an inner-city working-class community – the Cregagh estate in Belfast – but was much, much more than a promising talent. The small and skinny but precocious kid with stardust in his boots was discovered by Manchester United scout Bob Bishop, as if he was prospecting for gold and had discovered El Dorado. "Boss," Bishop excitedly told United manager Matt Busby, "I think I've found you a genius."

The promise came true. Best moved to Manchester, got homesick and went back to Belfast, returned a fortnight later, and proceeded to tear up English and European football. Many players shared some of his qualities but few, if any, could combine them to such devastating effect. He was fast, two-footed, good in the air and could finish as well as anyone. He was elegant, balanced, a slinking dribble of mercury who would twist defenders around until they were dizzy. His close control was phenomenal, his shooting prowess exceptional and he was strong in an age when flair players were the target of merciless, cynical treatment. Best could look after himself and emerge from the battle with the ball still glued to his magical feet.

It all served United famously well, with a raft of trophies owing much to Best's beautiful style and lethal purpose. But something else was going on. As the 1960s began to get into full permissive swing, Best became one of the decade's poster boys. He was good-looking and, for all his reserve – or probably because of it – a compelling figure people were attracted to regardless of whether they were football fans or not. His dark hair grew longer; he was dubbed "El Beatle" by the Latin media after one particularly brilliant performance in the European Cup against Benfica in 1966. He would return to haunt the Portuguese side in the 1968 European Cup final, jinking around goalkeeper José Henrique to score the second goal in United's epic 4-1 win.

It was Best's high-water mark. While he was playing scintillating football, other distractions had taken hold. He had been fined by a concerned Busby for late night partying during the 1965–66 season, and the nightclubs, women and booze began to take an increasingly firm grip on his life. At first it was all part of the Best legend, his sexual conquests winning him even more admirers. The boutiques, flash cars and bespoke designer homes seem like a cliché now but represented a revolution at the time. Best had first emerged in a time of monotone grey, but at his peak he played in glorious technicolour, on and off the field.

But his lifestyle predictably caught up with him. Struggling to cope with the unceasing attention (press and fans were in virtually permanent camp outside his house) and a United side in decline, Best's own form suffered. After Busby left, the fractures with United deepened as Best missed training and matches, only to be found in some bolthole or other, seemingly always with a Miss World to keep him company. He quit Old Trafford in 1974, dabbled in a short but entertaining comeback at Fulham and a glitzy cameo in America, before a meandering series of often bizarre one-off appearances with a variety of teams.

It left an almost desperate sense of frustration about Best. He never got to play in the World Cup

> *He has ice in his veins, warmth in his heart, and timing and balance in his feet.*
>
> Danny Blanchflower

Club	Appearances	Goals
Manchester United	470	179
Stockport County	3	2
Fulham	47	10
Hibernian	22	3
Bournemouth	5	0

Country	Appearances	Goals
Northern Ireland	37	9
TOTAL	**584**	**203**

Honours

League Title	2 (1964–65, 1966–67)
European Cup	1 (1968)

FOOTBALL
-STATS-

George Best

Name: George Best
Born: Belfast, 22nd May 1946
Died: 25th November 2005
Position: Winger/midfielder
Playing career: 1963–83

for one, as Northern Ireland failed to qualify throughout his time in the green shirt. He retired from playing far too soon, but had much to offer as a perceptive judge and pundit – when he was sober, that is. Repeated public displays of drunkenness had turned him from a glamorous young icon into a middle-aged has-been whose antics could be pitiful. Everyone wanted to buy Best a drink, but it resulted in a sad spectacle for those who really knew him and those who had seen him in his prime.

A recovery of sorts came with an extended period on Sky Sports commenting on the elite and star-studded strand of entertainment he had done much to influence. His addictions could not be beaten, however, and after a liver transplant, his health failed again and he died in 2005. He was just 59. But while there was a huge feeling of loss at his passing, there were also many, many invaluable memories of a footballer quite unlike any other.

Best was one of the most photographed of all footballers, whether it was to capture his grace on the field or his headline-generating off-pitch exploits.

While he was rightly renowned for his phenomenal control on the deck, he was also adept in the air, scoring with a powerful header against West Brom in 1967 (left). By then he had already been dubbed "El Beatle" thanks to his demolition of the mighty Benfica in their own back yard, and his mischievous decision to don a sombrero on the return to England in March 1966 (below left).

Glamorous girlfriends such as Susan George (below) and hanging around swanky boutiques began to become a bigger part of Best's life as he fully embraced the spirit of the 1960s (opposite above left). A comeback of sorts came with a briefly brilliant sojourn with Fulham, alongside Rodney Marsh and Bobby Moore (opposite main) but Best's prime as a player had already passed. He was still big box office and hung out with stars such as Billy Connolly (opposite above middle). It was a far cry from his days under the tutelage of Sir Matt Busby, who had been something of a father figure to the young Northern Irishman (opposite above right).

George Best and Susan George on holiday in Palma Nova, Majorca, June 1969.

> *We had our problems with the wee feller, but I prefer to remember his genius.*
>
> Sir Matt Busby

Alcohol and Best became inseparable as his career came to a premature end. In 1972 he went AWOL from Old Trafford before the end of the season, taking refuge in a Marbella hotel. Best did return to United but it was the beginning of the end of the most famous of all careers that had begun on the streets of Belfast in 1948 – a tiny wee boy with a football at his feet.

Ron Harris (right) suitably unimpressed after a clash with QPR's Stan Bowles in 1974. Harris would later manage Bowles at Brentford.

RON HARRIS

A loyal Chelsea legend and a hero of The Shed, Ron "Chopper" Harris ranked among the most renowned and feared hardmen, in an era when they were in their prime.

When a player's nickname is "Chopper" – and it is still said today with a great deal of wistful affection – it reveals much about the individual and the era in which he played. In a period when the genuine football hardmen could ruthlessly intimidate their opponents, few struck as much terror into those players as Ron Harris. Tellingly, he also had their respect, for Harris was a fine player and Chelsea's most dedicated and long-serving son.

Hailing from the East End along with his brother Allan, who also played for Chelsea, Harris made the switch to West London to be a key member of the Blues' FA Youth Cup-winning squad in 1961. The step up to the senior ranks came in the next season and promotion to Division One, as manager Tommy Docherty began his recasting of the side. Harris would remain in position for almost the whole of the next 18 years – a model of consistency, rugged purpose and wholehearted commitment to the cause.

He won the League Cup in 1965 and as skipper led Chelsea in four subsequent major finals. His and that vintage Chelsea side's finest hour came in the 1970 FA Cup, and the shuddering clashes with Leeds United over the drawn final and the replay. These two games did much to inspire the long-standing and fierce rivalry between the two clubs. Both were blessed with talent in abundance but also hard, gritty players and tough characters.

Harris was pre-eminent among this specialist group, going toe-to-toe with a Leeds team who were no strangers to the more physical side of football. Harris' challenge on Eddie Gray early on in the replay – and one which effectively rendered the Scotsman a spectator – was a key determinant in the outcome of the game.

Fair means or foul? Harris and his kind walked a fine line between honest endeavour and darker tactics, but there was an integrity about the way they operated: players knew what they were going to get when they faced people like Harris. Not just raw and uncompromising tackling but also an opponent who refused to be beaten.

Such determination enabled Harris to become the first Chelsea captain to lift the FA Cup. He followed that up with another first just a year later – the European Cup Winners' Cup, Chelsea's debut continental trophy. The rot soon set in at Stamford Bridge, however, as the club experienced financial hardship, and this inevitably had a knock-on effect on the team. Players came and went but Harris stayed loyal – a remarkable 21 years in total – from when he joined as a youth, even when he lost the captaincy to Ray Wilkins. Harris finally left in 1980 for a three-year spell as player-manager at Brentford, and after a very brief period as Aldershot boss, retired from the game.

Harris reportedly used to call his parents mummy and daddy well into his adult years which added a somewhat jarring element to his image, but off the field he was and remains an ebullient character popular with team-mates and foes – and a hero to Chelsea fans.

Chopper in full-blooded action, challenging Crystal Palace's Peter Taylor in February 1976.

Club	Appearances	Goals
Chelsea	795	14
Brentford	61	0
TOTAL	**856**	**14**

Honours
FA Cup	1 (1970)
League Cup	1 (1965)
European Cup Winners' Cup	1 (1971)

FOOTBALL —STATS—

Ron Harris

Name: Ronald Edward Harris

Born: Hackney, 13th November 1944

Position: Full-back

Playing career: 1961–83

> *I've never been late for anything in my life. Except the odd tackle.*
>
> Ron Harris

Harris receiving congratulations as a member of the England Youth team which won the Junior World Cup in 1963.

109

> " I like to think I've something else to offer apart from being a bit of a butcher. "
>
> Ron Harris

Capturing that special moment for posterity in a phone booth at Piccadilly station. By beating Leeds in an epic and bruising encounter, Chelsea won the FA Cup for the first time, with Harris the proud skipper.

RIGHT: You're off: Harris gets his marching orders from referee Reeves during a 1973 meeting with Brighton.

BELOW: Harris (far right) joined by (left to right) George Graham, John Hollins and Terry Venables, as they hear the news that Chelsea had drawn holders Liverpool in the first round proper of the FA Cup in 1965.

BILLY BREMNER

The central figure in one of the great postwar English sides, Billy Bremner was competitive, tough and a model of inspirational leadership for both club and country.

> " *He could tackle, score goals and spray passes all over. Billy Bremner was some player.*
>
> Charlie Nicholas "

At just 5ft 5in, Billy Bremner didn't exactly have the bearing of a midfield enforcer, but that didn't stop him being one of the most fierce competitors in the game and the heartbeat of Leeds United's greatest-ever side. Both player and club deserved more trophies, while Bremner's all-round qualities should not be overshadowed by his reputation as a tigerish tackler.

Ultra-competitive Bremner certainly was, but he needed to be to thrive in the cauldron of English League football's midfield during the 1960s and 1970s, when every club had its battlers and bruisers. Born in Stirling, a place integral to the psyche of Scotland's national identity, Bremner was plucked away from the big Scottish clubs that were eyeing him up, to join Leeds directly from school. He made his debut in January 1960 and featured alongside another player nearing the end of his career, Don Revie.

Revie would of course go on to manage the Yorkshire side from 1961 and utterly transform it from Division Two also-rans into the country's leading club. Bremner was Revie's right-hand man in the grand plan and integral to Leeds' success. Indeed he was often dubbed the manager's second son, but that did not suggest a yes man who would simply do as his boss demanded. Revie trusted Bremner to lead on the field and he did so with great distinction. An illustration of his fearless attitude came in a famous

> " He was only a wee man, but he was a heavyweight player.
>
> Ron Yeats "

After going close a number of times, Leeds finally won the League in 1968–69. Bremner showed off the trophy to a huge and ecstatic crowd at a civic reception.

Club	Appearances	Goals
Leeds United	772	115
Hull City	61	6
Doncaster Rovers	5	0

Country	Appearances	Goals
Scotland	54	3
TOTAL	**892**	**124**

Honours

League Title	2 (1968–69, 1973–74)
FA Cup	1 (1972)
League Cup	1 (1968)
Inter-Cities Fairs Cup	2 (1968, 1971)

Billy Bremner

Name: William John Bremner

Born: Stirling, 9th December 1942

Died: 7th December 1997

Position: Midfielder

Playing career: 1960–78

confrontation with Dave Mackay, when he kicked his compatriot on the leg Mackay had twice broken. An enraged Mackay picked up the young Bremner by the scruff of his neck, with Bremner the picture of innocence.

That willingness to confront players with big reputations served Bremner well as Leeds went on to win an overdue League title in 1968–69 with cup glory to follow and successes and near misses in Europe. Bremner was at the heart of it all, winning possession, launching attacks and contributing his fair share of goals. Leeds earned a kind of infamy among some critics for their supposed win-at-any-cost approach, with Bremner cast as chief villain. To Leeds fans, though, he was a hero, and a flame-haired darling to the Elland Road crowd. Similarly for the Scottish national side, Bremner was an all-action inspirational presence, winning 54 caps and leading the side to an unbeaten campaign in the 1974 World Cup, though not progressing past the group stages.

After 16 years at Leeds, he completed his playing career with stints at Hull City and Doncaster Rovers, where he served his managerial apprenticeship (and returned for his final job in the game). In the meantime, his old club had suffered a marked decline and in 1985 he answered the call to come back to revive Leeds United's fortunes. In this he was only a partial success, one of many to ultimately fail in restoring Leeds to the big time. That would finally be realized under Howard Wilkinson, but Bremner was to the end a Leeds legend. His untimely death from pneumonia at just 54 ended an energetic and fully-committed life, both on and off the pitch, and was marked by the placing of a statue in his honour just outside the stadium.

Leeds manager Don Revie (right) and Bremner (centre, next to coach Syd Owen) grab a bite to eat before leaving for London to play Chelsea in the 1970 FA Cup final. Leeds lost, but would go on to win the competition two years later.

Bremner familiarly in the thick of it, this time after a fracas with Manchester United, March 1965 (left and below). In later years he and Kevin Keegan had an infamous punch-up in the 1974 Charity Shield that saw both players get their marching orders.

> He had a heart the size of Elland Road.
>
> Eddie Gray

LEFT: In 1987 Bremner showed all the determination as Leeds manager that he had displayed as a player.

Southampton's Hugh Fisher presents a floral peace offering to a suitably amused Hunter in January 1974.

NORMAN HUNTER

When Norman "bites yer legs" Hunter was in his prime and taking on opponents, there was usually only one winner. His dedication to winning did much to inspire the great Leeds side of the era.

Another victim feels the full force of Hunter's uncompromising style. Referee Bob Matthewson reaches for his pocket to book Hunter after his foul on Palace's John Craven in November 1972.

There's a memorable incident from a wintry 1968 meeting between Everton and Leeds United, when the ball was pinging around in the midfield. As Everton's Howard Kendall tried to launch an attack, a figure clad all in white came blitzing through the centre circle to leave Kendall in a crumpled heap. Moments later, the Everton man was carried from the field, dazed, confused and just about coming to his senses. All that was missing were a few cartoon birds flying around his head.

It was Norman Hunter who was responsible for Kendall's temporary befuddlement. Of all the legendary hardmen of the 1960s and 1970s, it was Hunter who was arguably the toughest. His Leeds and England team-mate Jack Charlton may have had his little black book featuring the names of his intended targets, but Hunter had no need for such paperwork. He simply carried out his job with near-lethal effectiveness.

It seems remarkable now that Leeds nearly passed up the opportunity of signing the teenager from Gateshead, believing he was too lightweight. But new boss Don Revie had other ideas and saw him as the ideal centre-half partner for Charlton. The pair became one of the most effective and feared partnerships, as Leeds enjoyed their most successful ever period. "The Grim Sweeper" was integral to it – making tackles, distributing the ball cleanly and efficiently and coming up with the odd goal into the bargain.

Along the way, the Hunter legend grew. He formed a number of on-field rivalries that have themselves passed into folklore. He and Peter Osgood had a long-running enmity, but one laced with mutual respect and good humour. There were few laughs when it came to little Francis Lee, however. He and the much taller Hunter famously came to blows during a tempestuous clash between Leeds and Derby County in November 1975. The ill-matched pair traded punches in a protracted fight before being sent off.

Hunter later regretted the fight with Lee, but such escapades cloud his all-round effectiveness. He was tough, no doubt, but could also play. Opponents may have gone to bed with nightmares of having to face him, but they also recognized his talent, never better illustrated than when Hunter won the first ever PFA Player of the Year award in 1974.

At international level there was not quite the same degree of recognition, nor success, with Charlton and Bobby Moore rendering Hunter a squad player rather than a first-team pick. Bitter disappointment came in the World Cup qualifying game against Poland in 1973, when Hunter's mistake led to the Poles scoring, which effectively meant that England would miss the 1974 finals. Hunter was left inconsolable.

He eventually left Leeds after 14 years for a three-season spell at Bristol City, then a largely successful stint as player and later manager at Barnsley, before a variety of coaching jobs including a very brief caretaker spell back at Elland Road. It was on his old stomping grounds that Hunter became a popular matchday host, and a summarizer on local radio, offering predictably blunt and forthright but honest views on the game that were always worth listening to.

Club	Appearances	Goals
Leeds United	726	21
Bristol City	108	4
Barnsley	31	0

Country	Appearances	Goals
England	28	2
TOTAL	**893**	**27**

Honours

League Title	2 (1968–69, 1973–74)
FA Cup	1 (1972)
League Cup	1 (1968)
Inter-Cities Fairs Cup	2 (1968, 1971)
World Cup	1 (1966)

FOOTBALL –STATS–

Norman Hunter

Name: Norman Hunter
Born: Gateshead, 29th October 1943
Position: Defender
Playing career: 1962–82

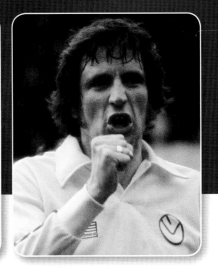

Hunter acclaims Alan Clarke's winner in the 1972 FA Cup final.

As he is sent off and led away from the fray, Hunter looks on in what would be a forlorn hope to see his Leeds side prevail in the 1973 European Cup Winners' Cup final against AC Milan. In this tumultuous match Leeds had goals disallowed, penalty appeals turned down, Hunter unfairly dismissed and eventually lost the game to an indirect free-kick which was taken directly. Referee Christos Michas was later found guilty of match-fixing and banned by UEFA from officiating for life.

" *You never intentionally went out to hurt anyone, but that will to win became so strong and you'd get wound up and the red mist would come down sometimes.* "

Norman Hunter

COLIN BELL

Nicknamed "Nijinsky", Colin Bell was a thoroughbred forced to retire too early, but still ranks as Manchester City's greatest ever player.

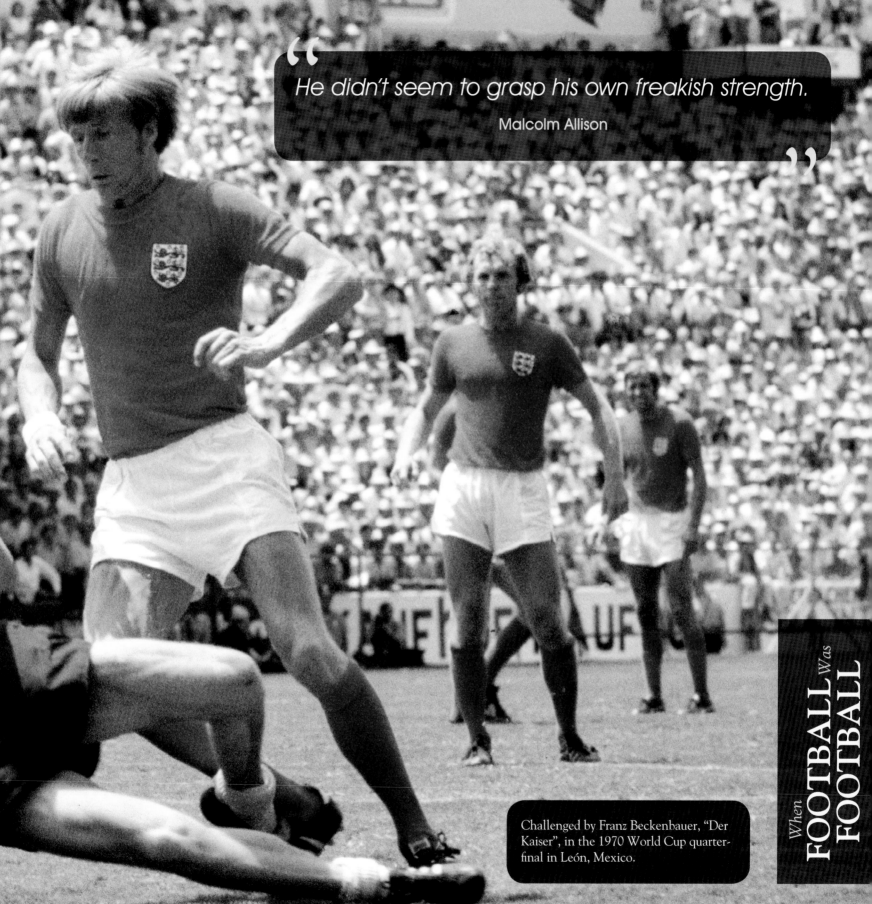

He didn't seem to grasp his own freakish strength.

Malcolm Allison

Challenged by Franz Beckenbauer, "Der Kaiser", in the 1970 World Cup quarter-final in León, Mexico.

When FOOTBALL *Was* FOOTBALL

123

While he was in his regal pomp during the late 1960s and into the 1970s, Colin Bell was dubbed the "King of the Kippax" in honour of his standing among the faithful who thronged the huge terrace at Manchester City's old Maine Road home. Nowadays a stand at City's gleaming new home is named after him. Both tributes are testament to the enduring appeal Bell has among City supporters and the integral part he played in the history of the club during one of its most successful periods.

Had he not been forced to effectively retire at just 29, Bell may well have gone on to even greater accomplishments for his club and the national side. For Bell was a wonderful all-rounder whose range of qualities made him one of the great midfielders of his time.

He began his professional career just north of Manchester with Bury, where his performances excited Malcolm Allison, assistant manager at City under Joe Mercer. On Big Mal's recommendation, City signed Bell and he made an immediate impact, becoming a fundamental part of the side that would go on to win trophies at home and in Europe.

He cost just £47,000, which has to be one of the great bargain buys. In a three-year period City won five major trophies, with Bell the driving force. His speed, strength and stamina were phenomenal, as he covered every blade of grass with unrelenting energy. His runs from deep brought goals galore – a ratio of almost one in every three games, which represents a phenomenal strike rate for his position.

The praise and the plaudits flooded in, in contrast to Bell's own quiet modesty. He was called up to the national side in 1968 but the consensus is he was never really given a full opportunity for England, his cause not helped by a series of managerial changes. He was arguably at his best in a Three Lions shirt when Mercer took over as caretaker boss in 1974, but thereafter did not receive the number of call-ups his quality surely merited.

Back at Maine Road, he suffered greater misfortune. A tackle with Manchester United's Martin Buchan in a League Cup tie in 1975 left Bell with a serious knee injury that he never really recovered from. When he attempted a comeback in 1978, one City fan, Dave Brammer, was so overjoyed that he ran on to the pitch to place a crown on Bell's head as he warmed up. The roar of the crowd that greeted Bell was one of the most heartfelt ever witnessed.

But such acclaim was not enough. After a handful of appearances in two troubled seasons, Bell tried for a revival in the NASL, but finally admitted defeat in 1979 aged 33.

In later years he returned to Manchester City for a couple of coaching jobs in addition to charity work. In 2006 there came a remarkable and poignant twist. Bell's mother had died young from a bowel tumour when he was just an infant. When a specialist surgeon Jim Hill read about this in Bell's autobiography, *Reluctant Hero*, he recommended Bell should have an examination. A benign but potentially life-threatening tumour was discovered and successfully removed.

"
Better than Best.

Manchester City fans' t-shirt
"

LEFT: Getting ready to compete in TV's *Superstars* show in July 1974. Bell was an all-round athlete who could have thrived as a middle-distance runner.

BELOW: The 19-year-old Bell (bottom left) with Bury team-mates Bob Owen, Alec Lindsay and Jimmy Kerr. This photograph dates from January 1966, shortly before Bell's transfer to Manchester City.

Club	Appearances	Goals
Bury	86	25
Manchester City	492	152
Country	**Appearances**	**Goals**
England	48	9
TOTAL	**626**	**186**

Honours	
League Title	1 (1967–68)
FA Cup	1 (1969)
League Cup	2 (1970, 1976)
European Cup Winners' Cup	1 (1970)

FOOTBALL
–STATS–
Colin Bell

Name: Colin Bell
Born: Hesleden, 26th February 1946
Position: Midfielder
Playing career: 1963–79

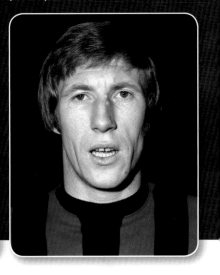

BELOW: Bell's stellar talent was in contrast to his unassuming character. Seen here with the 1975 England squad trying on their new sunglasses, Bell (centre) kept a low profile.

LEFT: Celebrating in the away dressing room at Newcastle United with George Heslop, as City become Champions in 1968.

BELOW: Giving Arsenal the runaround in November 1969.

> " Colin Bell was unquestionably a great player, and I don't use the word 'great' lightly. "
>
> Bobby Charlton

Man about town: Rodney Marsh, then at QPR, and looking very sophisticated in London in November 1969. The only trouble was that he was all dressed up to make a disciplinary appearance before the FA after receiving three bookings, which resulted in a four-week suspension.

RODNEY MARSH

One of the leading lights in the new breed of maverick footballers of the late 1960s and early 1970s, Marsh was an extravagant and gifted individual, and one of the era's most entertaining players and personalities.

It somehow seemed like destiny that George Best and Rodney Marsh would end up playing together. Though it would come in the latter years of both of their careers, and was only short lived, it was in some respects the perfect combination: Best the original pop-star footballer, Marsh the maverick clearly influenced by his contemporary, but a highly-individual and magical, extravagant talent in his own right.

Marsh played the game and conducted his lifestyle very much off the cuff. That did not endear him to a number of his managers and some supporters, but it thrilled other fans captivated by his fluid, very un-English style and highly distinctive approach. Combined with his looks and enthusiastic embrace of the pleasures to be had off the pitch, Marsh became a cult hero whose career and lifestyle any number of young men aspired to.

One reason for Marsh's fondness for fun no doubt stemmed from his childhood. Raised in an impoverished family in London's East End, with a docker father who named his son after the battleship HMS *Rodney*, Marsh had a tough, often violent upbringing, and found an escape through football. When local club West Ham passed up the opportunity to sign him, Fulham pounced to bring him to Craven Cottage for the first of two spells beside the River Thames. Injuries hampered him and after a dispute with manager Vic Buckingham, Marsh was transferred to Third Division neighbours Queens Park Rangers in 1966.

There he flourished, his talent and tricks given a free rein in an electric season that saw him score 44 goals and win the League Cup for the club against the odds in 1967. Promotion followed and then another step up the League as a vibrant Rangers side with Marsh at its heart reached Division One.

They could not retain their place, however, but it wasn't until 1972 when he was 27 that Marsh got the big-club move his talent deserved. League-leaders Manchester City claimed his signature with a £200,000 transfer fee, with manager Malcolm Allison reasoning that Marsh's flamboyance would secure another Division One title. Instead they finished fourth.

Marsh's part in this decline has been pored over and debated ever since. The player himself has admitted his arrival was a key factor. Whatever the full truth, Marsh did go on to perform well for City and win legions of devoted fans, but amid frequent changes in management, and rows with one of the incumbents, Tony Book, his departure was inevitable. It resulted in a move to the sunny surroundings of Florida and the Tampa Bay Rowdies, where Marsh seemed to have found his natural home. He was tanned, supremely self-confident and flash, but he had the means to

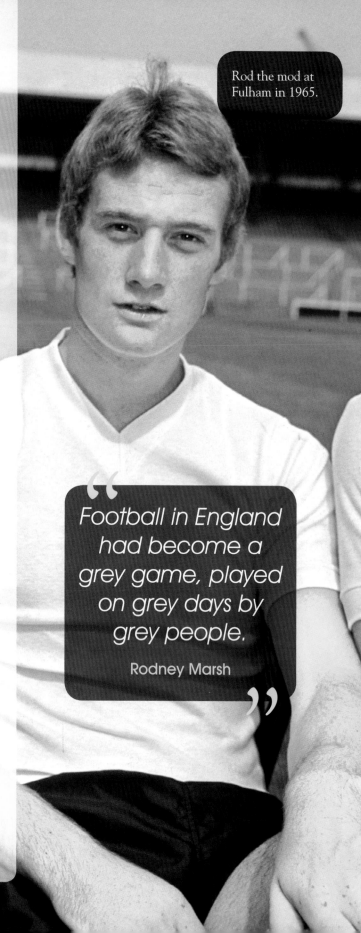

Rod the mod at Fulham in 1965.

> "Football in England had become a grey game, played on grey days by grey people.
>
> Rodney Marsh"

Club	Appearances	Goals
Fulham	90	28
QPR	242	134
Manchester City	152	47
Country	Appearances	Goals
England	9	1
TOTAL	493	210
Honours		
League Cup	1 (1967)	

FOOTBALL –STATS–

Rodney Marsh

Name: Rodney William Marsh
Born: Hatfield, Hertfordshire, 11th October 1944
Position: Forward
Playing career: 1962–76

live up to the billing. The great Alfredo di Stéfano even commented that Marsh was the most gifted footballer outside of Brazil.

There was an all-too-brief cameo back at Fulham alongside Best and Bobby Moore, before a return to Florida, where he played his last match in 1979. Marsh subsequently had a series of coaching jobs in the US, took a sports psychology degree and became chief executive at Tampa before leaving the game.

It brought to an end what many regard as an unfulfilled career. Marsh only played nine times for England – his was a personality that was far too wayward and individual for the still very traditional national set-up, particularly when it came up against the stern and no-nonsense form of Alf Ramsey – while the NASL's gain was surely Division One's loss. Marsh was often at odds with authority and he displayed a maddening mix of football brilliance one minute and frustrating over-elaboration the next. But he played the game the way he loved it – wanting to bring colour and excitement rather than safe, reliable but boring predictability.

That outlook has been evident in his life since retiring from the sport. Often outspoken, his attitude has earned and lost him a number of media pundit roles. He was something of a natural for reality TV shows, notably *I'm a Celebrity Get Me Out of Here!*, where his avuncular, straight-talking style made for compelling viewing. Fifty years on he was still entertaining the crowds.

Sharing a cuppa with England team-mates Bobby Moore and Mike Summerbee in 1972. Marsh was too much of a nonconformist to really make it with the England national side.

RIGHT: Signing on the dotted line at Maine Road. The pensive faces of Marsh, City manager Malcolm Allison and chairman Eric Alexander were a foretaste of topsy-turvy times to come in Manchester.

129

Living the American dream
(complete with vodka bottle) in
Tampa Bay, 1978.

"
People loved him.

Malcolm Allison

"

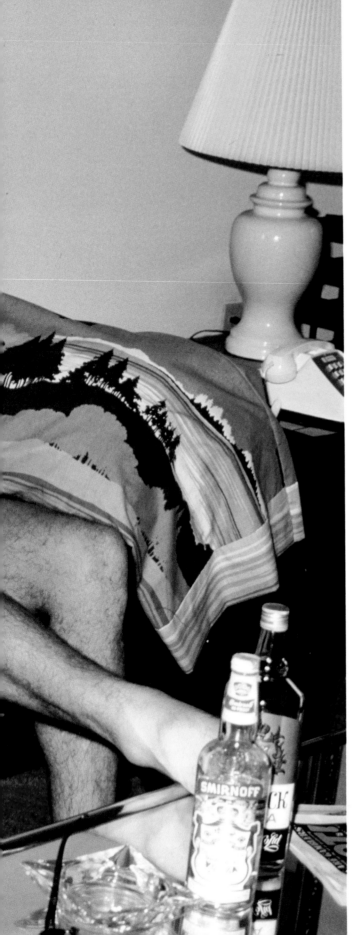

ABOVE: Back at Fulham for a brief spell in 1975, Marsh teamed up with George Best for one of the dream attacking pairings.

BELOW: The playboy image at the Playboy Club in 1973, alongside Mick Channon.

PETER OSGOOD

The darling of the Shed End was the frequent target of the hardmen and hatchet merchants, but emerged from his battles as a sublime master of the goalscoring craft. He was the uncontested "King of Stamford Bridge".

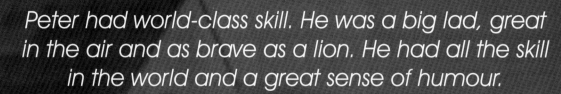

> *Peter had world-class skill. He was a big lad, great in the air and as brave as a lion. He had all the skill in the world and a great sense of humour.*
>
> Tommy Docherty

LEFT: The King in his castle: Osgood holds off the challenge of Arsenal's Frank McLintock, with Stamford Bridge's Shed End in the background, 1970.

BELOW: Osgood (left) and fellow scorer John Dempsey showing off the European Cup Winners' Cup to ecstatic fans down the King's Road. Chelsea beat the mighty Real Madrid 2-1 in a replayed final in Greece.

Of all the faces of the 1970s that stick in the football fan's mind, the image of Peter Osgood is one of the more memorable. Whether careering through the mud to unleash an unstoppable shot, the net bulging from a bullet header, a delicate finish, or a full-blooded confrontation with a defender intent on inflicting bodily harm, the striker was one of the most identifiable players of the period – and now one of the most missed.

The man affectionately known as Ossie was a gifted practitioner of the striker's craft. He had technique and finesse allied to strength, speed and determination. In footballing parlance he could also look after himself. Balanced and poised, he had natural ability in abundance but would also work hard for the cause.

That cause was primarily in the service of Chelsea. He was born in natural Blues territory in Windsor, and swiftly made his mark, earning his debut at just 17. Elevated to a regular first-team spot he scored prolifically, gaining a place in Alf Ramsey's longlist squad for the 1966 World Cup. As the new youthful Chelsea took shape, Osgood was at its heart. A broken leg meant he missed out on the club's first ever FA Cup final in 1967, but he returned to spearhead what was then Chelsea's most successful period.

Ossie scored in every round of the semi-final 1970 FA Cup run. After the first drawn final on a quagmire of a Wembley pitch came the titanic replay battle at Old Trafford, where Osgood's bullet of a headed equalizer provided the competition with one of its most iconic goals. He added to the memory bank with a goal in the 1971 European Cup Winners' Cup final against Real Madrid and another in the replay.

For all such glittering successes, however, there is a lingering sense of a career unfulfilled. Osgood might have been part of the eventual England 1966 World Cup squad, but missed out due to his broken leg. In truth, that spared Ramsey from having to make the decision to omit Osgood. He would play only four games for

the national side, twice as a substitute. It was a pitiful return for such a prodigiously talented player, his class all but ignored by an England management suspicious of forthright temperaments.

Osgood's character – not quite as rebellious as the likes of Best and Marsh but not far off – didn't suit the England set-up. He was much more at home down the King's Road with the Chelsea set, out on the town celebrating with the famous and the glamorous.

This in turn, however, caused problems at Stamford Bridge and ructions with manager Dave Sexton who finally tired of Osgood's perceived attitude, alongside that of his team-mate and socializing soulmate, Alan Hudson. Both were put on the transfer list, with Osgood despatched to Southampton for £275,000.

Sexton said he might regret it and for a few seasons, Osgood proved that doubt was well placed. While Chelsea were to slide, the Saints thrived, winning the FA Cup in 1976. Osgood took the well-worn route to the USA for a time, before returning

as the prodigal son to Stamford Bridge for a brief but unsuccessful swansong. Chelsea were in definite decline and a pale shadow of the side Osgood had once graced.

In retirement Osgood ran a pub back in his native Windsor alongside old team-mate Ian Hutchinson, and proved to be a charming matchday hospitality host (after run-ins with then Chelsea owner Ken Bates). Ossie was also a natural as an after-dinner speaker, recounting tall tales of his heyday. He died aged just 59 after a heart attack while attending a family funeral. He remains the "King of Stamford Bridge".

Club	Appearances	Goals
Chelsea	380	150
Southampton	161	36
Norwich City (on loan)	3	0

Country	Appearances	Goals
England	4	0
TOTAL	**548**	**186**

Honours

FA Cup	2 (1970, 1976)
European Cup Winners' Cup	1 (1971)

FOOTBALL –STATS–

Peter Osgood

Name: Peter Leslie Osgood

Born: Windsor, 20th February 1947

Died: 1st March 2006

Position: Forward

Playing career: 1964–79

LEFT: Alan Hudson and Osgood were central figures at Chelsea but were ushered out of the door after disputes with manager Dave Sexton – Hudson to Stoke, Osgood to Southampton – and faced each other in their new club colours in 1974.

BELOW RIGHT: Under the slightly bemused eye of Dave Sexton, Osgood (third from left) got the hairdryer treatment alongside team-mates Dave Webb, Marvin Hinton, Charlie Cook and Tommy Baldwin. They were joined by comedian Marty Feldman at the opening of a wig boutique and hairdressers in Chelsea, in November 1969.

BELOW LEFT: Ossie opening his own fashion boutique in June 1972.

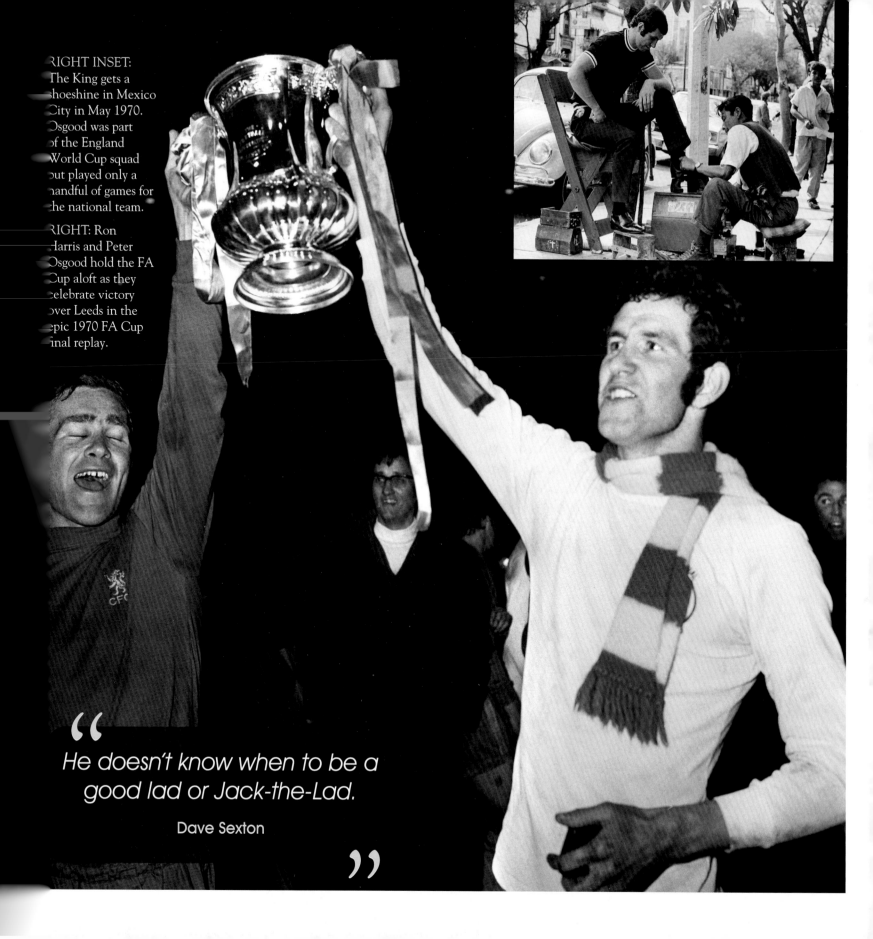

RIGHT INSET:
The King gets a shoeshine in Mexico City in May 1970. Osgood was part of the England World Cup squad but played only a handful of games for the national team.

RIGHT: Ron Harris and Peter Osgood hold the FA Cup aloft as they celebrate victory over Leeds in the epic 1970 FA Cup final replay.

> " *He doesn't know when to be a good lad or Jack-the-Lad.* "
>
> Dave Sexton

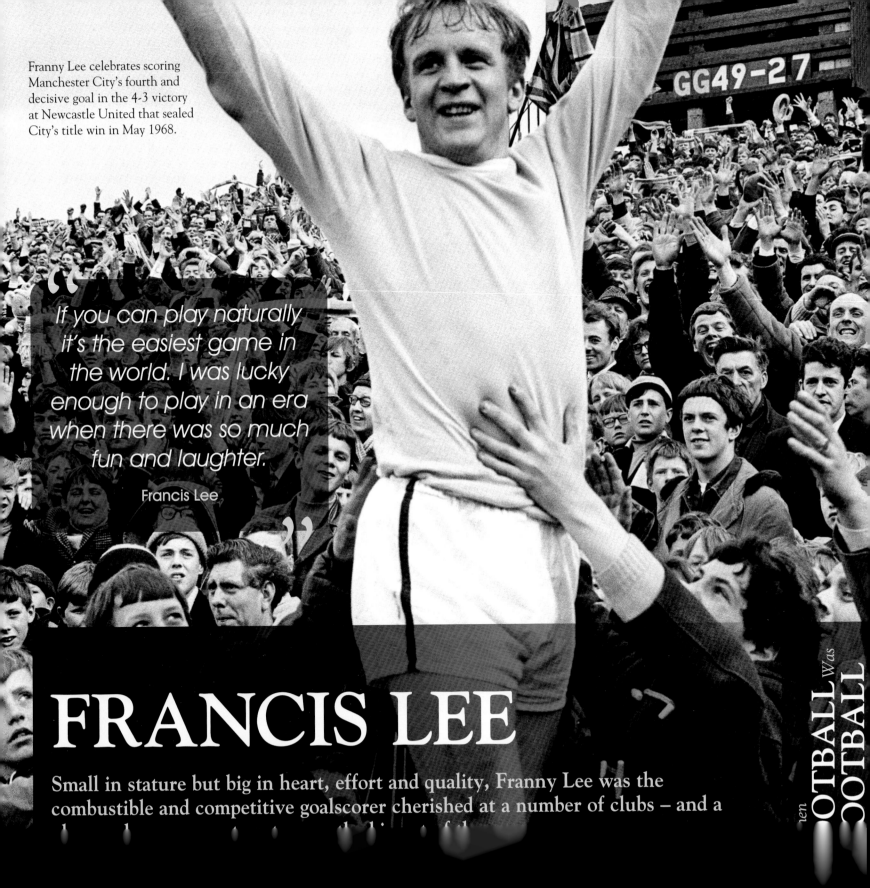

Franny Lee celebrates scoring Manchester City's fourth and decisive goal in the 4-3 victory at Newcastle United that sealed City's title win in May 1968.

GG49-27

> "If you can play naturally it's the easiest game in the world. I was lucky enough to play in an era when there was so much fun and laughter."
>
> Francis Lee

FRANCIS LEE

Small in stature but big in heart, effort and quality, Franny Lee was the combustible and competitive goalscorer cherished at a number of clubs – and a

"Lee Won Pen" ran the joke at the time: it was coined in dubious honour of the supposed tendency of Franny Lee to go down far too easily in the box and earn regular penalties for his side. Yet for all the controversy surrounding his approach, Lee was a striker whom colleagues and fans loved to have on their side. Small but stocky, he was game for a contest with anyone, and invariably came out on top. That will to succeed later served him well in a business career that even had him occupying the chairman's seat at Manchester City.

It was at City that Lee had his finest hours. He won four trophies on the trot under the Joe Mercer and Malcolm Allison managerial double act – the League, the FA Cup and then the League Cup and European Cup Winners' Cup. In a team brimming with talent and power, Lee seemed to embody both attributes.

These qualities were first honed at Bolton Wanderers. Lee played for six years at Burnden Park, his reputation as a barrel-chested penalty area predator attracting the attentions of other clubs. It was Manchester City who took the plunge, investing a club record £60,000 in 1967 for what Mercer hoped would be the final piece of the jigsaw as he and Allison assembled that great City side.

The promise came true. Lee's 16 goals in 31 appearances helped propel City towards the title, then further glory in succeeding years. He was top scorer at Maine Road for five out of seven seasons, including the 1971–72 campaign in which he became the first player to top 30 for a League season since Peter Doherty in 1936–37. Among those goals were no fewer than 15 penalties in all competitions, a remarkable stat that fuelled accusations that he went looking for fouls.

This was before the modern age, when the art of winning a penalty is an almost accepted part of the game. Back in the 1970s, it was a serious accusation and one that Lee was at pains to deny. It was a reputation that followed him when he was sold by City – against his wishes – to Derby County in 1974.

Once again he was pivotal to a team winning the Championship, his 33 goals that season playing a major part in Derby's title triumph. In November 1975 came the famous clash with Norman Hunter (see page 119) after the Leeds man accused Lee of securing and scoring a penalty by foul means. The fury of Lee in the subsequent punch-up was a vivid illustration of how he viewed such accusations. It also showed what a fearless competitor he was, in physically standing up to the much taller Hunter.

Such a combative and determined streak was to serve him very well indeed in retirement. Lee had always had an interest in business,

Lee is escorted off the field by his Derby manager Dave Mackay, sporting a split lip after his unforgettable confrontation with Norman Hunter of Leeds in November 1975. Both players were sent off.

"My brother always said you'd have to be mad to be a manager. What other job is there where your livelihood depends on 11 daft lads?"

Francis Lee

encouraged by his father. He was savvy enough to negotiate his own deals, reportedly making him the best-paid player in the country when he joined Derby for £1,000 a week, and in contrast to many of his peers who struggled to adapt to life after playing, Lee thrived in the outside world. He made several fortunes in such diverse activities as manufacturing toilet rolls and training racehorses.

Such proven acumen made him a strong candidate to enter the newly commercialized world of club football which arrived with the advent of the Premier League. As City struggled to rediscover past glories, Lee took over from the reviled Peter Swales. The task of reviving City had been a thankless one, as they had been left behind by other clubs seizing upon new financial opportunities.

"Forward with Franny" became the fans' rallying cry. Unfortunately though, the club went backwards. Lee was not a success as chairman, his promises of a new golden age underlining his ineffective managerial choices. It was an unhappy time as City plunged further down the League, and Lee resigned in 1998.

But it did not tarnish Lee's reputation as a genuine City great, nor his legacy at his other clubs, where fans still fondly remember his colourful and unforgettable goalscoring exploits.

Club	Appearances	Goals
Bolton Wanderers	210	106
Manchester City	330	148
Derby County	83	30

Country	Appearances	Goals
England	27	10
TOTAL	**650**	**294**

Honours

League Title	2 (1967–68, 1974–75)
FA Cup	1 (1969)
League Cup	1 (1970)
European Cup Winners' Cup	1 (1970)

FOOTBALL
–STATS–

Franny Lee

Name: Francis Henry Lee

Born: Westhoughton, 29th April 1944

Position: Forward

Playing career: 1960–76

LEFT & BELOW: Franny the family man: with wife Jean in 1975 and son Gary in 1968. Gary is seen here swigging from a bottle of pop as his dad sat in the bath at Maine Road with injured full-back Bob Kennedy.

> " If cups were awarded for cock-ups, you would not be able to move in City's boardroom. "
>
> Francis Lee

In typically competitive action for England in the 1970 World Cup, pleading his innocence after a challenge on Brazil keeper Félix.

LEFT: Lee 1 (pen). Scoring from the spot to help City towards triumph against Górnik Zabrze in the 1970 European Cup Winners' Cup final.

BELOW: Arriving as the hoped-for saviour back at Manchester City, this time as chairman in 1994. It didn't quite go to plan.

> *When he plays on snow, he doesn't leave any footprints.*
>
> Don Revie

Eddie Gray, a wizard on the wing and anywhere else on the field, evades a tackle from Everton's Mike Bernard in March 1976.

EDDIE GRAY

A magician on the pitch and the model of one-club loyalty, Eddie Gray was a player of great elegance and skill who lit up the game across three decades.

At Elland Road they carry a torch for a select band of players. The great John Charles and Billy Bremner rank high, while the likes of Jack Charlton, Johnny Giles and Norman Hunter feature among a star-studded list. But there is a special place reserved for Eddie Gray. While neutrals might not fully appreciate the extent of Gray's talent, in West Yorkshire there is no such lack of awareness.

Gray was a maestro, a cultured wide player who would drift and wander, probe and create. He was nimble, sure-footed, blessed with outstanding close control and flawless technique. All these attributes and more were summed up in one extraordinary match against Burnley in 1970. After scoring with a long-range cracker, Gray went even better in the second half. Winning the ball out on the left by the goal-line, and faced with almost half the Burnley team, he shimmied, twisted, dragged the ball back, dropped his shoulder and swerved his way through increasingly desperate Burnley tackles, before arrowing a right-footed drive into the net.

It was one of the great goals and so appropriate that Gray should score it. He was not a great harvester of goals – scoring once every eight matches or so – but those he did get were often beautiful to behold. Furthermore, he was the architect of so many other goals scored by team-mates. In an age long before stats for assists, Gray was the great provider.

He had been tempted from Glasgow to Leeds as a youth, despite his hankering to play for Celtic. Jack Charlton had reportedly said after a practice match that the club had to sign the kid so he wouldn't have to play against him. Gray's rise was rapid, swiftly becoming a mainstay of Don Revie's emerging side. He was there for the trophy triumphs and the frequent frustrations, as Leeds missed out on the greater number of honours they should have won. The team had a reputation for physicality and ultra-professionalism – "dirty Leeds" was a lasting label – but if this perhaps did the club a disservice, it certainly belittled how good Gray was. An indication of how integral he was came in the 1970 FA Cup final against Chelsea. He had been a major influence in the first game, to the extent that Chelsea hatched a special plan to nullify the effect of Gray in the replay. Ron Harris' sustained and unpunished physical treatment effectively crippled Gray and put him out of the game.

This was no isolated incident. Gray had been on the receiving end of the rough stuff for many seasons – he had carried a long-standing thigh problem from his teenage years – but successive injuries began to take their toll. It resulted in a severely truncated international career. At club level, his extended absences from the side were personally costly – he missed out on a second League title medal in 1973–74 – and for the team. With his career in the balance as the legacy of injury hit home, he was

"
I fell in love with the football club.

Eddie Gray on Leeds
"

made a sub by new manager Jimmy Armfield for the 1975 European Cup final which ended in a highly controversial defeat that still rankles with Leeds fans to this day.

It proved to be the last hurrah for that great team, but Gray stuck by the cause through the bitter disappointments of relegation and financial woes. Indeed he has stayed loyal throughout the decades of occasional highs and frequent turmoil, stepping in as manager and caretaker when called upon. He has coached at various times at several levels at Elland Road, and was more recently made a club ambassador. No one could be a better ambassador than Eddie Gray.

Club	Appearances	Goals
Leeds United	577	68

Country	Appearances	Goals
Scotland	12	3

TOTAL	**589**	**71**

Honours

League Title	1 (1968–69)
FA Cup	1 (1972)
League Cup	1 (1968)
Inter-Cities Fairs Cup	2 (1968, 1971)

FOOTBALL -STATS-

Eddie Gray

Name: Edwin Gray

Born: Glasgow, 17th January 1948

Position: Forward

Playing career: 1966–84

LEFT: The ultimate Leeds loyalist: behind the manager's desk during his stint in the early 1980s.

RIGHT: Domestic bliss: Gray with his wife Linda, five-month-old daughter Fiona and dog Khyber, April 1970.

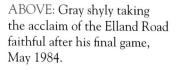

ABOVE: Gray shyly taking
the acclaim of the Elland Road
faithful after his final game,
May 1984.

RIGHT: In action against
Bobby Lennox and his boyhood
favourites, Celtic, in the
European Cup semi-final second
leg, April 1970.

> *He was easily the best player that I ever played with. He had tremendous ability.*
>
> Gerry Francis

Bowles celebrating his 1974 international call-up by Alf Ramsey in suitably individual style.

STAN BOWLES

Fans loved him, some of his managers did, and so did most of his bookmakers: Stan Bowles is one of the great lovable rogues of English football.

While the talent of Stan Bowles is widely recognized, there are many who feel he didn't fully exploit his special gift. It is a charge that is perhaps unfair: Bowles played well over 500 games over a period of 17 years, and while there were no meaningful trophies to show for it, he left fans with some of their most cherished football memories, whether it was for a sublime piece of skill on the ball or a colourful escapade away from the action.

He was a bold, streetwise Mancunian kid who became a cult hero in London, most notably at QPR. He might – perhaps should – have been a natural star at Manchester City. He scored twice on his debut but that was about as good as it got. Instead of thriving under the enlightened leadership of Joe Mercer and Malcolm Allison as their great City side blossomed, Bowles withered, clashing with Allison before being sent packing. There were some eye-catching displays during a short tour of various clubs down the League until Bowles was taken down south with QPR, then an ambitious Second Division club looking for a player who had that little something different to offer.

Rangers needed a replacement for Rodney Marsh. Other players had demurred, reasoning there were too many expectations to live up to, but Bowles had no such qualms. Club and player clicked. As Rangers enjoyed what would be a golden period in their history, Bowles was centre stage. He was a team player but also a rare individual talent – the sorcerer bewitching opposition defences with his incisive passing, penetrating runs and often spectacular goals.

But it wasn't simply what Bowles did so much as the way that he did it. He had style, flair, charisma and a carefree but confident attitude towards life that showed itself in the way he played. While he was getting up to various off-field tricks and capers, and making front-page headlines, he was playing a major part in Rangers' assault on the bigger clubs and mounting a genuine title challenge.

Under the shrewd management of Dave Sexton, the club came agonizingly close to achieving that dream in the 1975–76 season when they were just pipped by Liverpool. It was QPR's high point and Bowles' too. After a falling-out with new boss Tommy Docherty, he switched to Nottingham Forest and came under another highly idiosyncratic boss in Brian Clough.

Predictably, things didn't work out and there was a return to London with Leyton Orient, and then three final years back in the west of the capital with Brentford. Amid this peripatetic journey around the clubs of England, Bowles squeezed in a

As he was such a skilful player, Bowles was inevitably a target for practitioners of the cruder footballing arts, as with this painful incident during a March 1975 derby against Chelsea.

Club	Appearances	Goals
Manchester City	21	4
Bury	5	0
Crewe Alexandra	51	18
Carlisle United	36	13
QPR	318	97
Nottingham Forest	19	2
Leyton Orient	44	7
Brentford	81	16

Country	Appearances	Goals
England	5	1
TOTAL	**580**	**158**

FOOTBALL –STATS–

Stan Bowles

Name: Stanley Bowles

Born: Manchester, 24th December 1948

Position: Forward/midfielder

Playing career: 1967–84

Bowles had a fear of flying, forcing him to take the train back alone from a game at Newcastle in January 1976.

Bowles checks the form in the search for a hot tip in the racing pages.

> *People say to me: 'Who is the best player that you've ever played with?' Well, Stan would rank with some of the best.*
>
> Frank McLintock

handful of England appearances. He was never likely to be comfortable in the confines of the national set-up, but it was a measure of his talent that three different managers picked him, even if they couldn't quite make his selection work.

Since retirement, Bowles has become something of a poster boy for the 1970s game. The tales of blowing thousands on dodgy nags, carousing and womanizing continue to entertain but they can't match the sheer thrill of Bowles the footballer in free-flowing action. Stan really was the man.

149

The darling of Loftus Road getting a less-than-generous reaction from visiting Manchester United fans.

> *I told him I would rather trust my chickens with Colonel Sanders.*
>
> Stan Bowles when told "you can trust me" by Tommy Docherty

151

MALCOLM MACDONALD

Though he was a player very much of the 1970s, Malcolm Macdonald was like a centre-forward of old – so strong, powerful and prolific that he earned the nickname "Supermac".

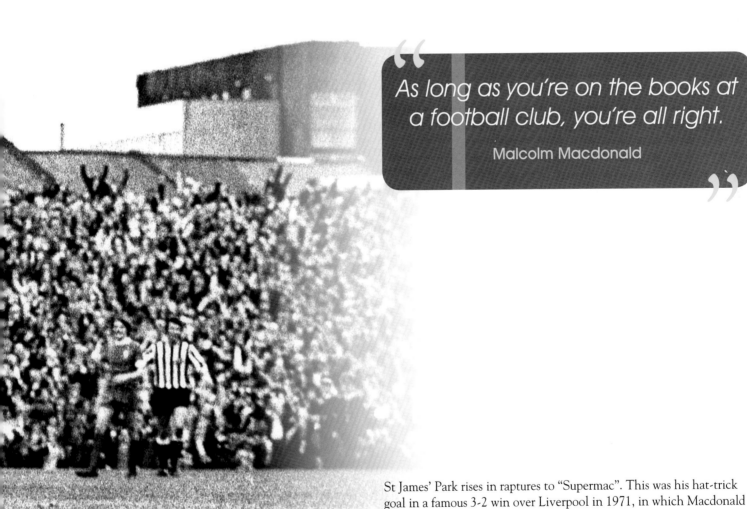

> " As long as you're on the books at a football club, you're all right.
>
> Malcolm Macdonald "

St James' Park rises in raptures to "Supermac". This was his hat-trick goal in a famous 3-2 win over Liverpool in 1971, in which Macdonald made his home debut.

The number 9 shirt has a special place in every football team, but few clubs value it as much as Newcastle United. Whoever bears the number has a strong pedigree to live up to. Goalscoring heroes like Hughie Gallacher and Jackie Milburn laid down a standard that has been tough for many strikers to attain. Malcolm Macdonald, however, had no such problems. With his physical strength and his technical expertise, he filled the role of hero striker to perfection.

It wasn't just at St James' Park where Macdonald shone. He was a one-in-two goalscoring success at Fulham, Luton Town and Arsenal, and had a brief but productive spell with England. But it was in the north-east that he enjoyed his best times, becoming an adopted Geordie whom Newcastle fans still revere and celebrate to this day.

Born in West London, he was initially taken on as a left-back at his local side Fulham by then manager Bobby Robson, before being converted to a striking role. Within a year he was on the move to Luton. There his speed, skill and lethal shooting brought him a prolific goal record and drew the attention of bigger clubs. Macdonald traded in the invaluable currency of goals, making him a prized asset, for which Newcastle were prepared to pay £180,000 in 1971.

Manager Joe Harvey was looking to reinvigorate a United side whose progress had stalled after winning the Fairs Cup in 1969. Further trophies would prove elusive – a recurring theme of Newcastle's history ever since – but despite the lack of silverware, Macdonald's five-year spell was a spectacular one. His home debut couldn't have been scripted any better, the barrel-chested young Londoner cracking in a hat-trick against Liverpool in a famous 3-2 win.

Thereafter the goals continued to flow. He was top scorer for Newcastle for five consecutive seasons. At international level, Macdonald only played 14 games but rattled in almost one goal every game for England, chiefly through a remarkable and record-equalling five against Cyprus in 1975.

Once again, other clubs came calling and Macdonald headed back to London and Arsenal in 1976 for a fee of £333,333. He looked set to establish himself a Highbury favourite as beloved as he had been at St James' Park, but picked up a bad knee injury two seasons in and never fully recovered. An attempt to rebuild his career in Sweden proved futile and, at just 29, Macdonald was forced to quit the game.

" *Reporters can make or break footballers. The reverse can rarely be said.*

Malcolm Macdonald "

Scoring for Arsenal against his old club Newcastle, 1976.

Club	Appearances	Goals
Fulham	13	5
Luton Town	101	61
Newcastle United	257	138
Arsenal	108	57

Country	Appearances	Goals
England	14	6
TOTAL	493	267

FOOTBALL –STATS–

Malcolm Macdonald

Name: Malcolm Ian Macdonald
Born: Fulham, January 7th 1950
Position: Striker
Playing career: 1968–79

ABOVE: As manager at Fulham in 1983, Macdonald was prepared to get his hands dirty helping to roll out turf for the new pitch at Craven Cottage.

LEFT: Macdonald's England career was brief. Manager Don Revie (centre) was not the striker's biggest fan and it was claimed he even said to Macdonald he had only selected him due to pressure from the press.

It was an understandably heavy blow. While Macdonald went on to manage, he later became increasingly dependent on booze to numb the severe pain that was a legacy of his injuries. Four relatively successful years as boss of Fulham were followed by a disastrous season in charge of Huddersfield Town, which included a 10-1 thrashing by Manchester City. He left and his problems mounted, with divorce and then bankruptcy adding to his woes.

Supermac's public decline revealed what could happen to footballing superheroes once their playing days were over. His experience was not an uncommon one. But showing the same determination he had done on the pitch, he battled back to carve out another career in the media. A thoughtful and intelligent presenter and commentator, he articulates what it is like to have played the game to such a high standard – and fondly recalls his days as a legendary number 9.

RIGHT: In explosive action for Newcastle United.

BELOW: Macdonald was given his chance in professional football by then Fulham boss Bobby Robson. The pair had met years before when Macdonald was an eight-year-old Fulham fan who had asked Robson for his autograph when he was still a player. The youngster even carried Robson's bag to the ground and talked excitedly about the sport, which Robson recalled when he signed Macdonald as a teenager.

KEVIN KEEGAN

Kevin Keegan was a hugely successful player with a big personality that translated well to a high-profile – if not always happy – managerial career.

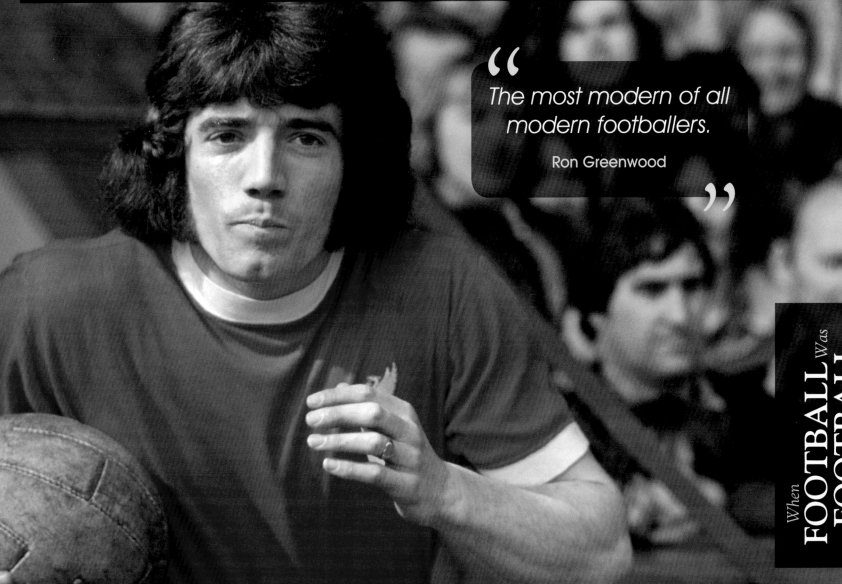

" *The most modern of all modern footballers.*

Ron Greenwood "

Kevin Keegan has been a part of the English football landscape for five decades. Whether as an elite club player (most notably at Liverpool), an international with England or as a manager at both levels, he has been in the spotlight almost continuously. He has adopted a lower profile in recent years, but still stands as one of the game's most emblematic and charismatic figures.

Industrious in his style and passionate in his attitude towards the game, it was often said of Keegan that while he was not perhaps a naturally gifted player, he worked feverishly hard and made his talent go a very long way. Undaunted by a couple of frustrating rejections by Doncaster Rovers and Coventry City, he fought his way through the ranks at Fourth Division Scunthorpe United, performing well in a struggling team.

Such endeavour did not go unnoticed and the scouts soon came calling. It was Liverpool and Bill Shankly who made the decisive move, signing Keegan for a fee of £35,000 in 1971. Shankly later described it as "robbery with violence", so high was Keegan's eventual worth to the Merseysiders. Forming a wonderful partnership with John Toshack, Keegan was instrumental in Liverpool's rise to immortality in the 1970s. His goals, tenacity and teamwork helped the club to League titles, FA and UEFA Cups and, once Bob Paisley had replaced Shankly, the ultimate prize of the European Cup in 1977.

In the process, Keegan became a Liverpool legend and a darling of the Kop. Player, club and fans formed a remarkable bond, with Keegan later admitting he would be so caught up in Anfield's unique atmosphere that he would sometimes be in tears during games.

But there was more prosaic method to Keegan's effectiveness. He was skilful but not prodigiously so. Instead he had a knack for being in the right place at the right time, to both spot and seize an opportunity. It was an admirable characteristic which he utilized in his activities away from playing. If George Best was the first superstar footballer, Keegan was the first to fully exploit the opportunities such fame presented. He was comfortable as a face for advertising, selling or promoting everything from aftershave to showing kids how to cross the road safely. He rubbed shoulders with prime ministers, had a solo hit record with 'Head Over Heels' in 1979 and was rarely off the TV screens.

His willingness to constantly seek new opportunities resulted in a move to Germany for a record £500,000 in 1977, and three successful years with Hamburger SV. In an era when English footballers either played safe and stayed at home or took the American dollar in the glitzy but low-standard NASL, Keegan dared to be different and tested himself in a highly competitive foreign league.

It paid off with Hamburg's first League title in a generation and twice resulted in Keegan being named European Footballer of the Year. He missed out on another European Cup when Hamburger SV were beaten in the final by Nottingham Forest in 1980, but by then his status had been elevated to global renown. Looking for a move back home, he was the subject of an audacious scoop by Southampton manager Lawrie McMenemy.

After two happy years at Southampton, Keegan finally got the chance to play in a World Cup when England qualified for the competition for the first time in 12 years. Keegan had been an able servant for the national side, but unfortunately it came during one of the side's least successful periods. It was cruel luck that he was dogged by injury in the build up to Espana '82, and in the end he only featured for 20 minutes, missing with a header against hosts Spain that resulted in a 0-0 draw and an exit from the competition.

It was tough on Keegan, but he was reinvigorated by a move to Newcastle United.

Club	Appearances	Goals
Scunthorpe	141	22
Liverpool	323	100
Hamburger SV	111	40
Southampton	80	42
Newcastle United	85	49

Country	Appearances	Goals
England	63	21
TOTAL	**803**	**274**

Honours

League Title	3 (1972–73, 1975–76, 1976–77)
FA Cup	1 (1974)
European Cup	1 (1977)
UEFA Cup	2 (1973, 1976)

FOOTBALL
–STATS–

Kevin Keegan

Name: Joseph Kevin Keegan

Born: Armthorpe, 14th February 1951

Position: Forward

Playing career: 1968–84

BELOW LEFT: Hugged by an adoring fan, Keegan and his Liverpool team-mates, alongside manager Bill Paisley, go on an Anfield lap of honour after winning the League title in April 1975.

> *Everything I've done, I've done with enthusiasm and passion.*
>
> Kevin Keegan

He arrived in a blaze of glory, scored goals aplenty as Newcastle were promoted to Division One and then departed in spectacular style in a helicopter from the St James' Park pitch just moments after the final whistle of his final game.

It seemed that was that, with Keegan vowing not to go into management and preferring a leisurely life on Spanish golf courses. But his enthusiasm for the game and a challenge had him making the headlines with a return to Newcastle in 1992 to take over as manager. It was a rollercoaster of a reign as he first rescued the club from relegation to the old Third Division, gained promotion and then built an expensive, expansive side that came within a whisker of winning the Premier League. Ultimately it ended in disappointment, but Keegan's tenure gave the Toon Army their most cherished recent memories.

He was not able to repeat the feat in later moves to Fulham, Manchester City and an ill-chosen return to Newcastle that ended in acrimony and legal disputes. In the midst of these eventful times, Keegan had taken over as manager of the national side. Though he secured qualification for the 2000 European Championships, his 18 months in charge were not successful and Keegan resigned following defeat to Germany in the last game at the old Wembley.

The eventful second spell as Newcastle boss was Keegan's last foray into the frontline of football. Such is his celebrity and larger-than-life character, however, that he is still a prominent figure in the game. He may not have been the greatest player or manager the sport has seen, but he was certainly one of its most famous.

159

Keegan with perhaps the greatest Liverpool manager, Bill Shankly.

Starring at Hamburger SV.

> *Everything I've done, I've done with enthusiasm and passion.*
>
> Kevin Keegan

In the middle of a fine Southampton side including Chris Nicholl, Dave Watson, Mick Channon and Charlie George.

"Wor King Kev": becoming a hero at St James' Park.

LEFT: Splashing it all over with fellow Brut aftershave advert star, Henry Cooper.

161

CHARLIE GEORGE

George was a boyhood Arsenal fan who lived the dream by becoming a Double winner, and a footballer with a defined style and attitude.

Charlie George lies flat on his back, having just scored the winning goal in the 1971 FA Cup final for Arsenal.

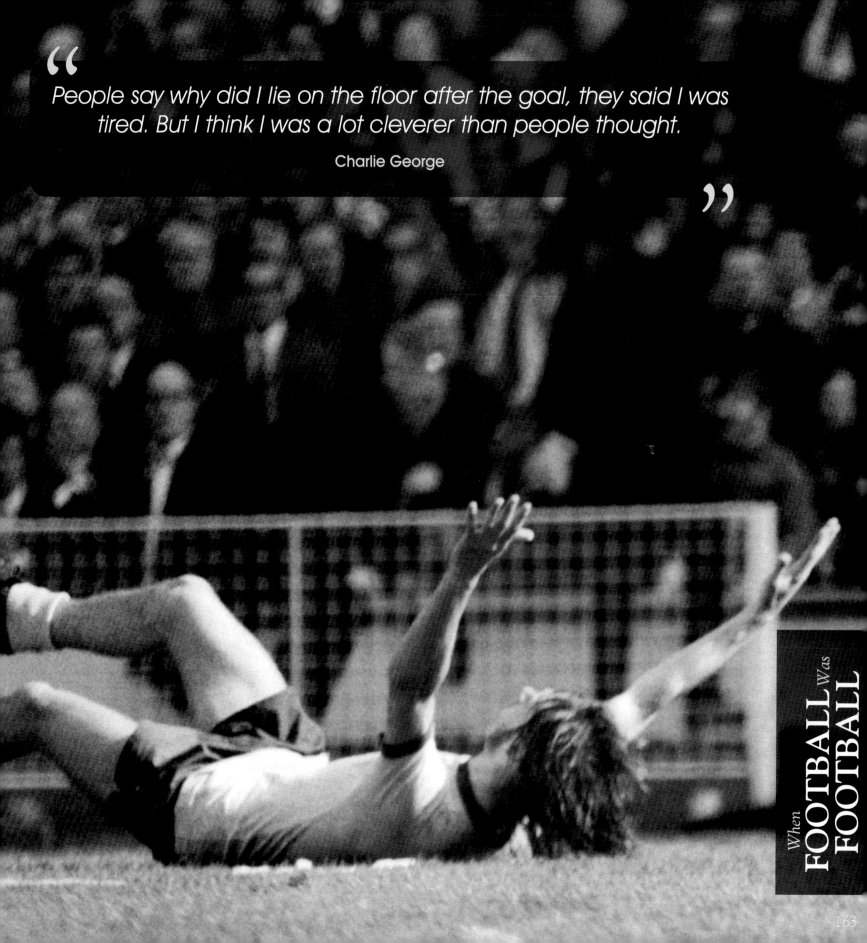

"People say why did I lie on the floor after the goal, they said I was tired. But I think I was a lot cleverer than people thought.

Charlie George
"

When FOOTBALL *Was* FOOTBALL

163

It is one of the FA Cup's most evocative images. A young, long-haired footballer noted for his supposedly laid-back demeanour has just scored a fantastic winning goal to seal a famous League and FA Cup Double for his club. He collapses to the floor, lying prostrate and smiling up into the sky. Not so long before he was a kid standing on the Highbury terraces and cheering Arsenal on. Now he was one of their legends.

Charlie George's winning goal in the 1971 FA Cup final – and his subsequent celebration – was his most notable contribution to the sport. There is a degree of disappointment that he didn't go on to achieve more, because his talent surely merited it. Playing for Arsenal in the early 1970s, a side that was built on organization and collective team effort, and in a League where physicality ruled, George's individualism and flair stood out. It did not quite gain him the achievements he could – or should – have earned, and meant he was a virtual stranger to international call-ups, but his style left his many adoring fans with a store of wonderful memories.

Born almost in the shadow of Highbury, George grew up as a committed Gunner. His upbringing turned him into a feisty character who baulked at taking unnecessary orders from authority figures. He was expelled from his secondary school where one of the part-time teachers was a certain Bob Wilson, who kept goal for Arsenal.

Wilson's club saw in the youthful George a troubled, unpredictable character, but one whose footballing talent was precious. As manager Bertie Mee developed his Double-winning team, he carefully nurtured George's gifts. It was not a seamless progression. Mee's disciplinarian nature clashed with George's rebellious streak. He was punished for various indiscretions, one of which involved George feigning illness to drop out of a reserves match in order to travel as a supporter to see the first team in an away game.

George was the real deal – a proper fan who happened to play for the club. Such close identification with the Arsenal cause bore fruit in that famous 1970–71 campaign. He missed a good chunk of it thanks to a broken ankle, and found his place up front taken by Ray Kennedy. Dropping back into an attacking midfield role, he flourished. In phase one of Arsenal securing the Double, the title was won at – of all places – White Hart Lane. Then came that sweltering day at Wembley, extra-time

Club	Appearances	Goals
Arsenal	179	49
Derby County	147	56
Southampton	44	11
Nottingham Forest (loan)	4	1
Bournemouth	2	0
Country	Appearances	Goals
England	1	0
TOTAL	**377**	**117**

Honours		
League Title	1 (1970–71)	
FA Cup	1 (1971)	
Inter-Cities Fairs Cup	1 (1970)	

FOOTBALL
–STATS–
Charlie George

Name: Charles Frederick George

Born: Islington, London, 10th October 1950

Position: Forward/midfielder

Playing career: 1968–82

RIGHT: While George, Bob Wilson and Pan's People don't exactly look overjoyed at the prospect, they teamed up to perform 'Good Old Arsenal' on *Top of the Pops* in May 1971. The lyrics to Arsenal's FA Cup song were actually written by Jimmy Hill.

LEFT: Chef George during his spell at Derby County.

and a thunderbolt shot that led to an exhausted George spread eagled on the turf. Or perhaps he was just wasting a bit of time?

That great Arsenal side soon withered, though. George's tendency to find trouble continued with further fines incurred for on-field indiscretions. Part of the issue was that George would not buckle to foul play from intimidating opponents. Adhering to the credo of his Holloway youth to fight back when threatened, he gave as good as he got.

This, however, was at odds with a club that made a conspicuous virtue of respectability. George's form waxed and waned and he drifted in and out of the side, culminating in a move away from Highbury in 1975. At Derby he showed glimpses of his quality, but it was a short-lived honeymoon. Further clashes with authority followed, notably in a single appearance for England and a furious row with manager Don Revie, a regimental type who failed to exploit George's maverick quality. There were spells at Southampton and shorter stays at Nottingham Forest and Bournemouth.

By 1982 George's career was over. Given his exceptional talent, it was an unfulfilled one in terms of medals and appearances, but it did little to tarnish his reputation among his fellow Arsenal supporters. George was one of them and they still love him for it.

> **Hello Duke, meet King Charlie!**
>
> Arsenal's John Radford to the Duke of Edinburgh, before the 1971 FA Cup final

The darling of the North Bank, and the "King of Highbury".

England's number one.

> *"I played for 30 years, 20 with England, and I did it by setting goals.*
>
> Peter Shilton"

PETER SHILTON

England's record appearance holder ranks as one of the world's greatest ever goalkeepers – his dedication to his craft extending over four decades.

It takes a special kind of player to figure in well over 1,000 competitive games. It takes an even better one to do so at the top levels of club and international football. Peter Shilton was a goalkeeping phenomenon whose glittering career began just after the end of the maximum wage cap and ended as the advent of the Premier League ushered in eye-watering salaries.

Shilton dropped out of the top flight just as those riches began to flow, but he was one of the players who had sparked the sport's domestic revival that made such wealth possible. As part of the England 1990 World Cup side, he was the elder statesman in a team whose heroic failure in losing in the semi-final captivated so many and breathed life into a struggling game. He might not have turned on the tears like Paul Gascoigne did (see page 198) but his performances were a fitting reflection of his outstanding service for the national team.

To reach such heights, Shilton needed his array of natural talents but also almost obsessive hard work. There is an oft-told tale about the young Shilton that illustrated his determination to be a success. At 6ft he was not a tall goalkeeper and so would hang upside down from the banisters of his family home in Leicester to try to stretch his frame.

It was Leicester City who gave Shilton his initial break, so confident in his ability that they sold Gordon Banks to make room for the young upstart. He didn't disappoint: his unrelenting work on the training field resulted in an outstanding level of consistency. He was not a particularly agile keeper, but used his broad, muscular frame and impeccable technique to master his area.

By 1970 Shilton had gained his first England cap. Though his error was in part responsible for England failing to beat Poland and thus missing out on qualification for the 1974 World Cup, he recovered to make the position his own for much of the next 16 years, save for a spell when he was at first partial understudy to, and then alternated with, Ray Clemence. In the meantime his club career progressed, first with a record £325,000 fee for a keeper that earned him a move to Stoke City, before a switch across the Midlands to Nottingham Forest. It was at the City Ground under Brian Clough and Peter Taylor that Shilton enjoyed his greatest successes, lifting the major trophies that matched his status, and registering the clean sheets that win matches as much as goals.

ABOVE: Lifting the European Cup with Forest team-mate Trevor Francis, May 1979.

BELOW: Shaking the "Hand of God" just before kick-off in the extraordinary World Cup quarter-final against Argentina, Mexico 1986.

Club	Appearances	Goals
Leicester City	348	1
Stoke City	121	0
Nottingham Forest	272	0
Southampton	242	0
Derby	211	0
Plymouth Argyle	43	0
Bolton Wanderers	2	0
Leyton Orient	10	0

Country	Appearances	Goals
England	125	0
TOTAL	**1,374**	**1**

Honours

League Title	1 (1977–78)
League Cup	1 (1979)
European Cup	2 (1979, 1980)

FOOTBALL
–STATS–

Peter Shilton

Name: Peter Leslie Shilton

Born: Leicester, 18th September 1949

Position: Goalkeeper

Playing career: 1966–97

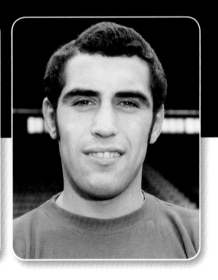

For England he was a dominant presence in both the 1982 and 1986 World Cups. In the latter he was on the receiving end of the twin faces of Diego Maradona: first with the infamous "Hand of God" goal, and then left helpless by the Argentinian's genius with the follow-up. This quarter-final reverse, however, did not damage Shilton's reputation and, having already passed Bobby Moore's appearance record of 108 caps, Shilton was still the world-class keeper whose dependability and experience were needed for the epic Italia '90 campaign.

That tournament marked the end of Shilton's international career, but he was still very much active in League football. After leaving Forest he had played for Southampton and Derby, before winding his playing days down with a combined managerial stint at Plymouth, a series of temporary stand-bys at number of clubs and then a final outing for Leyton Orient that saw him pass the 1,000 League appearances mark at the age of 47.

The world's media had gathered to see him achieve the feat and look back on his gilded career. It had not been all rosy. His period as Plymouth boss was turbulent, while stories about a gambling problem and an extra-marital fling resulted in front-page exposure. He never did get to play for one of the giants of the game that his quality should surely have entitled him to, but his extraordinary record over such a long period overwhelmingly speaks for itself.

> *What can I say about Peter Shilton? Peter Shilton is Peter Shilton, and he has been Peter Shilton since the year dot.*
>
> Bobby Robson

LEFT: Putting himself where it hurts for Southampton against Orient in January 1985.

BELOW: With England colleague Ray Clemence: the two vied for the England goalkeeping position until Shilton made it his own in the 1980s.

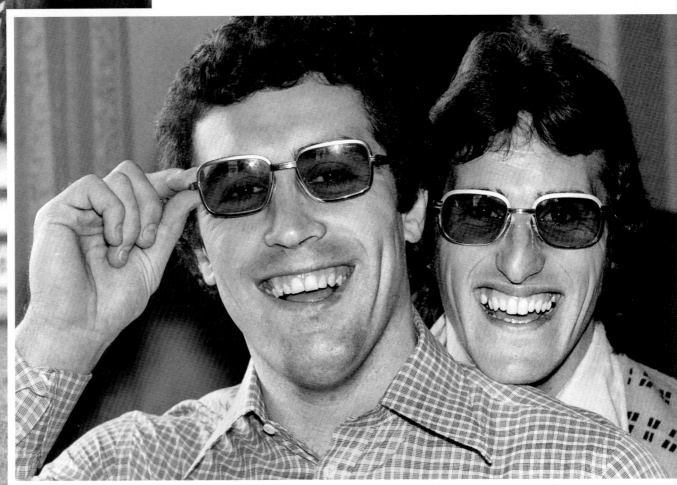

KENNY DALGLISH

A champion as a player and a manager, Kenny Dalglish was one of British football's greatest postwar figures, with a medal haul to match.

LEFT: Dalglish as a teenager at Celtic.

RIGHT: When you're smiling . . . Dalglish celebrates scoring yet another goal for Liverpool, this time against deadly rivals Manchester United at Old Trafford, February 1983.

"
Is he better in midfield or up front? Och, just let him on the park.

Jock Stein
"

Taciturn, guarded and dour are just a few of the descriptions used to describe Kenny Dalglish. While he may not have been one of the game's most emphatic communicators, his football and myriad achievements on the pitch have spoken far more eloquently than any soundbite. In the way he played – and then managed – he was one of the game's most expressive individuals.

Forever identified with Liverpool, it was north of the border that Dalglish had already made a huge name for himself. At Celtic, the boyhood Rangers fan had won four Scottish titles and four Scottish cups, as well as surging past the 100 League goals mark. So, when Bob Paisley brought him down south for £440,000 in 1977, Dalglish arrived with a big reputation. But he also had a big challenge ahead of him. Stepping into Kevin Keegan's boots at Anfield was no mean task. That Dalglish not only compensated for Keegan's absence, but made it redundant, illustrates the scale of his success. A fine player Keegan may have been, but Dalglish had the better talent and Liverpool benefited from it enormously.

The club and Dalglish won trophies with almost metronomic regularity. As Paisley's red machine powered into gear, Dalglish was its most finely engineered and efficient part. He lacked raw pace but, as the cliché goes, was a yard faster in his head. Operating between midfield and lead striker, he was the principal architect of Liverpool's attacking intent, dissecting defences with his passes, leaving them standing with his penetrating runs and maintaining a relentless pressure on their wits.

For the national side, too, Dalglish was a star. The limitations of Scotland meant he was never likely to replicate the trophy-winning success he enjoyed for his club, but his record 102 appearances and 30 goals are testament to his abilities and longevity on the international scene.

Dalglish scored goals – lots of them – but made even more. With a succession of front partners at Liverpool, in particular Ian Rush, he gave this magnificent Liverpool side its potency and penetration. Dalglish on song – and he was a model of consistency – was one of the emblematic images of 1970s and 1980s football.

Scoring the famous 1986 winner against Chelsea that secured the League title for Liverpool, Dalglish's first as a manager.

> *Don't talk to me about Dalglish. The only man on the pitch. Christ, what a player!*
>
> Bill Shankly

As was his beaming smile. Not for him the contrived goal celebration. Instead he displayed the joy of simply scoring and making goals. That evident happiness was reined in somewhat for the more businesslike nature of being a player-manager, but there was no let-up in the relentless success, with further triumphs both before and after he hung up his boots.

He had taken over as Anfield boss during one of the club's dark periods, in the immediate aftermath of the Heysel Disaster. Dalglish will also be remembered for his conduct in the awful time following the Hillsborough Disaster. Having witnessed such dreadful scenes, he and his players did immense good work for the club and community, attending funerals and strengthening the bonds between footballers and fans.

The enormous pressure that came with that job, however, eventually told on Dalglish, and after a nerve-shredding derby draw with Everton in 1991, he resigned. It seemed he would be lost to the golf course and newspaper columns. But just eight months later he was back in the game. He took up the manager's position at Blackburn, utilizing Jack Walker's

Club	Appearances	Goals
Celtic	322	167
Liverpool	515	172
Country	Appearances	Goals
Scotland	102	30
TOTAL	**939**	**369**

Honours

League Title	6 (1978–79, 1979–80, 1981–82, 1982–83, 1983–84, 1985–86 as player-manager)
FA Cup	1 (1986)
League Cup	4 (1981, 1982, 1983, 1984)
European Cup	3 (1978, 1981, 1984)

As a manager

League Title	4 (1985–86 as player-manager, 1987–88, 1989–90, 1994–95)
FA Cup	2 (1986, 1989)
League Cup	1 (2012)

ABOVE: Dalglish took over as Liverpool boss in 1985 from Joe Fagan (left), and thus continued the famous Anfield bootroom tradition laid down by Bill Shankly. Shankly had given Dalglish a trial as a teenager at Liverpool but the club had dithered over signing him, to Shankly's later regret.

FOOTBALL –STATS–

Kenny Dalglish

Name: Kenneth Mathieson Dalglish
Born: Glasgow, 4th March 1951
Position: Midfielder/forward
Playing career: 1969–90

millions to assemble another title-winning side, before taking on less successful tenures at Newcastle and Celtic.

There was also time for a short-lived return to Liverpool in 2011. By then the club had slipped down from the pinnacle of the English and European game. Dalglish had done so much to contribute to that ascent, so, when his second spell ended with dismissal, it did nothing to damage the mighty reputation of a truly great player.

ABOVE: Captaining Scotland in 1979 and shaking hands with the man he replaced at Liverpool, Kevin Keegan.

LEFT: Dalglish was a pivotal figure in rallying the club at the time of the Hillsborough Disaster in 1989. Twenty years later, he was joined by then manager Rafa Benítez for a memorial service at Anfield.

Pelé admiring the hair length of Trevor Francis during the Brazilian's visit to Birmingham in February 1972.

> "You looked at Trevor and saw everything you want as a footballer.
>
> Freddie Godwin, Birmingham manager "

TREVOR FRANCIS

Forever remembered as the first million-pound player, Trevor Francis was also one of the few British footballers who played successfully on the Continent.

In these days of £50m centre-halves and pay packets in excess of £350,000 a week, the impact created at the time by Trevor Francis' transfer to reigning champions Nottingham Forest seems almost quaint. In February 1979, after months of increasingly feverish speculation, Francis negotiated terms and signed on at the City Ground as the first million-pound British player. Remarkably, it came after Forest boss Brian Clough had agreed to let Francis play in the coming summer for NASL side Detroit Express – and gave him a run-out for the Forest third team in a local park before Francis had even put pen to paper.

Back in the English top flight, Francis was under huge pressure to live up to his price tag. Indeed Clough, in an echo of Jimmy Greaves' move to Spurs a generation before (see page 66), had tried to keep the fee below the symbolic £1 million. Fees, VAT and various add-ons ensured that would not be the case, but even if the price had not breached that totemic threshold, it was a burden for Francis to carry, since it was double the previous record.

On the whole, Francis did not quite live up to expectations. He would last only two seasons at Forest, with disagreements over his effectiveness and claims he was played out of position on the right instead of in a more central role. Yet for all the misgivings, Francis did make one emphatic contribution to justifying that fee. Just four months after the move, he was in the Forest side that had reached the European Cup final against Malmö of Sweden in Munich.

With seconds to go before half-time, John Robertson swung over a deep cross and Francis, racing at full pelt to meet it, flung himself low to head the ball into the roof of the net from an awkward angle.

It enabled Forest to complete a famous victory in the world's premier club competition. It was also indicative of Francis'

"
The best Englishman to have played in Italy.

Fabio Capello

"

The Million Pound Man: Francis signing for Forest and lurking in the background, with wife Helen and manager Brian Clough, and Clough's right-hand man, Peter Taylor.

Club	Appearances	Goals
Birmingham City	329	133
Nottingham Forest	93	37
Manchester City	29	14
Sampdoria	68	17
Atalanta	21	1
Rangers	25	0
QPR	32	12
Sheffield Wednesday	89	9

Country	Appearances	Goals
England	52	12
TOTAL	**738**	**235**

Honours	
European Cup	1 (1979)
League Cup	1 (1991)

FOOTBALL
–STATS–
Trevor Francis

Name: Trevor John Francis
Born: Plymouth, 19th April 1954
Position: Forward
Playing career: 1971–94

Celebrating after scoring the winning goal in the 1979 European Cup final.

athletic and technically proficient style. Such characteristics had made him a star at Birmingham City, the club he had joined from school in Plymouth. At St Andrews, Francis attained the status of hero for his goalscoring exploits – no fewer than 15 in his first 15 matches at the age of just 17 – and his all-round talent. That was what drew the attention of a number of clubs to try to sign him as he matured, and led to such an inflated price.

When things didn't work out as envisaged at Nottingham, he switched to Manchester City for an even bigger fee. That was a reflection of how highly managers rated him, but again it was a frustrating period, dogged by injuries. Francis was nothing if not ambitious, however. While he never lost that West Country burr, he was willing to take on new challenges and moved to Sampdoria in Italy, joining Graeme Souness as one of the new breed of trailblazing British players daring to test themselves abroad.

In five years in Genoa and then at Atalanta, Francis did not feature in a huge number of games, but he made a lasting impression. The technical Italian style probably suited him better than the more rudimentary English one. Nonetheless he was not done with Blighty just yet, enjoying brief run-outs with Rangers and then QPR and Sheffield Wednesday. He would manage both those English clubs for a spell, before returning like a prodigal son to the place where he would always be revered – Birmingham. In five years the Blues nearly realized the dream promotion their fans would have loved Francis to have achieved, but he could not quite pull off the task. Instead, after one last managerial job at Crystal Palace, Francis turned to media work.

It had been a career with its fair share of frustrations. The gifted youth had, for a number of reasons, never quite realized his full impressive potential. In terms of international football, 52 caps for England represented a fine achievement but left a nagging feeling that there should have been more. Ultimately Francis was perhaps not best suited to the English game of the time – £1 million price tag or not.

ABOVE: Back with his beloved Blues – this time as manager – and leaping for joy as his side score in a classic League Cup final in 2001. Birmingham eventually lost on penalties to Liverpool.

LEFT: Taking the acclaim of the fans at his new club, Manchester City, in 1981. Francis' stay at Maine Road was short and plagued with injury, before he left to try his luck in Italy.

> " There is no better player in the country than Trevor Francis.
>
> Alf Ramsey "

RAY WILKINS

A mainstay of a succession of club sides and a fixture in the England midfield, Ray Wilkins has been a high-profile figure in the game for over 40 years.

> " *It's better that someone does the talking for you and leaves you to do the playing.*
>
> Ray Wilkins "

LEFT: Making a splash with England at the Cima Club in Monterrey, Mexico, where the team was based before the 1986 World Cup.

BELOW: Wheeling away in celebration after scoring the best of his three goals for England. After chipping the ball forward to beat Belgium's offside trap, Wilkins then lobbed the goalkeeper to earn England a 1-1 draw in the 1980 European Championship match.

Tottenham's legendary skipper Steve Perryman once recalled seeing Ray Wilkins captain Chelsea as a 19-year-old, and sensed the immense pressure the youngster was under. Put in charge of a recently successful club fallen on hard times to fight what would be a losing relegation battle, it was a big burden to carry for any player, let alone a teenager.

But Ray Wilkins was a man who often took on responsibility. At a variety of clubs, both in Britain and abroad, he was a player team-mates could rely on and fans cherished. He was also a major player for England over a decade of service. At both levels he was often called upon to sacrifice his more natural game for the cause of the team, and did so with technical competence and gritty but professional determination. He wasn't nicknamed "Butch" for nothing.

Wilkins came from a footballing family. His father George played for Chelsea while brothers Graham, Dean and Stephen made the grade at differing levels. Ray joined his dad's side at a period when the Blues were one of the biggest and most successful clubs in the country. But by the time Wilkins made it into the senior ranks, Chelsea were in turmoil. Yet through the relegations, promotions, managerial upheaval and financial woes – and the stresses it inflicted on him – Wilkins was a model of stability on the field.

It was that consistency of top-level performance that drew the eyes of Manchester United, who brought Wilkins to Old Trafford in 1979 for a reputed fee of £777,777. His five years at United were successful. While the League title still eluded Ron Atkinson's team, a trophy eventually came in 1983 in the replayed FA Cup final, with Wilkins scoring one of the goals in the first game.

It was at United that "Butch" largely earned the dubious distinction of another nickname, "The Crab". It was penned to describe his tendency to pass sideways, reflecting the perception that Wilkins was more of a fetcher and carrier than a fluent, attacking midfielder. There was an element of truth to it, but it tended to overshadow fairer considerations of his all-round quality. Big clubs valued it highly, which is why he spent five years at United and why he became such an automatic pick for England.

Wilkins made his debut for the Three Lions in 1976 and was a key figure in ending the barren years of qualification failure, helping England finally take part in European Championships and World Cups once more. Again, he subsumed some of his own talent in service of the team, providing admirable back-up to Bryan Robson in the midfield engine room. His England career all but came to an end in

The Crab.

Ron Atkinson on Wilkins' playing style

Looking pensive as Chelsea skipper in the midst of a 3-1 defeat to West London rivals Fulham in 1977.

unfortunate circumstances: he was sent off after a second booking for dissent in a draw with Morocco.

Wilkins' obvious commitment was in part what appealed to AC Milan who signed him in 1984. His period at the San Siro came at a time when the club was in a relative trough, but he made a lasting impression. Years later, *Rossoneri* fans would still sing the Wilkins name in heavily accented English.

After a brief sojourn in Paris, Wilkins joined Graeme Souness' "Anglos" revolution at Rangers and prospered, before a return to England and something of an Indian summer to his career at QPR. He would go on to be player-manager at Loftus Road, winding down his playing days and then taking up a number of coaching roles, notably back at Chelsea where he was a highly able assistant to Carlo Ancelotti as Chelsea won the Double in 2010.

Dismissal from that role hit Wilkins hard. Indeed he has suffered from a variety of conditions and stresses throughout his career. But he has long flourished as a pundit. Erudite, informed and with an ability to convey the intricacies of the game with thoughtful insight, "Butch" brought all his wealth of experience into the TV studio to successful effect.

Club	Appearances	Goals
Chelsea	192	34
Manchester United	194	11
AC Milan	73	2
Paris St Germain	13	0
Rangers	94	3
QPR	208	11
Crystal Palace	1	0
Wycombe Wanderers	1	0
Hibernian	16	0
Millwall	3	0
Leyton Orient	3	0
Country	**Appearances**	**Goals**
England	84	3
TOTAL	**882**	**64**

Honours
FA Cup   1 (1983)

FOOTBALL
—STATS—

Ray Wilkins

Name: Raymond Colin Wilkins
Born: Middlesex, 14th September 1956
Position: Midfielder
Playing career: 1973–97

Wilkins was a powerful presence in the Manchester United midfield.

LEFT: Receiving congratulations after his stunning, curling strike in the 1983 FA Cup final against Division Two Brighton. The goal gave United the lead but the match ended in a draw, though United ran out comfortable 4-0 winners in the replay.

BELOW: Running the Rangers midfield in 1987.

IAN RUSH

Ian Rush was one of the most prolific of all goalscorers, who strengthened and maintained Liverpool's domination and played a major role in turning them into an even more potent and expansive side.

> *It's best being a striker.*
>
> Ian Rush

Rush, 95 minutes: scoring yet again against Everton, this time in the 1989 FA Cup final. Just five weeks after the Hillsborough Disaster, Liverpool's 3-2 victory was one of the sport's most poignant and moving triumphs. Rush would add a neatly headed second to seal a dramatic win.

Players who make a major impression on clubs these days invariably arrive to great fanfare and at enormous expense. Ian Rush had a rather more modest introduction to Liverpool. In the season they won their 12th League title, Rush was signed from humble Chester City for £300,000. It was big money – a record for a teenager – but the signing was marked down as one for the future and business as usual, reflecting Liverpool's steady way of doing things. Rush was sent back to Chester on loan for the next month and – if not quite ignored – slipped temporarily out of the limelight.

He would re-emerge to ensure his name would be lit up for the next 15 years or more with quite phenomenal feats of goalscoring. By 1996, when he left Liverpool – for the second occasion but this time for good – he had plundered a cumulative club record of 346 goals. It underpinned five League titles, several FA Cups and League Cups, a Double and a European Cup, and turned Liverpool into the most incisive force in club football, while making the man himself one of the all-time greats.

Though manager Bob Paisley had high hopes for his new signing back in 1980, the outward signs were not encouraging. The 18-year-old was tall, skinny and ungainly. He struggled to settle at first and there was talk of a possible transfer to Crystal Palace. But Paisley knew better and as he eased Rush into the first team, it soon brought dividends.

By the end of his second season, Rush had a League title winner's medal around his neck and 30 goals in the bag. The harvest of goals thereafter was unrelenting. Forming an intuitive, thrillingly effective partnership with Kenny Dalglish, Rush made opposing defences and goalkeepers seem redundant. A brilliant finisher, deceptively strong and powerful and with a supreme command of movement, timing and getting into the right position, Rush was a goal machine. It got to the stage that if he didn't score, it was a shock.

It led to a series of remarkable statistics: a sequence whereby Liverpool did not lose a game in which Rush scored for seven years; 32 League goals in 1984; records of five goals in FA Cup finals, the first Briton to win the European Golden Boot, 20 goals in Europe and 23 in Merseyside derbies for the boyhood Evertonian.

None of it seemed to go to Rush's head. He was quiet,

> *I wanted to stay on the pitch forever.*
>
> Ian Rush after his final Liverpool game

In action and at the centre of Everton's attention in 1990.

Club	Appearances	Goals
Chester City	39	17
Liverpool	660	346
Juventus	39	14
Leeds United	43	3
Newcastle United	14	2
Sheffield United	4	0
Wrexham	24	0
Country	**Appearances**	**Goals**
Wales	73	28
TOTAL	**896**	**410**

Honours

League Title	5 (1981–82, 1982–83, 1983–84, 1985–86, 1989–90)
FA Cup	3 (1986, 1989, 1992)
League Cup	5 (1981, 1982, 1983, 1984, 1995)
European Cup	1 (1984)

FOOTBALL –STATS–

Ian Rush

Name: Ian James Rush

Born: St Asaph, 20th October 1961

Position: Striker

Playing career: 1978–99

BELOW: Celebrating his fifth League title win with his Liverpool team-mates in 1990. This Liverpool side was rated by many as the best of the lot.

BELOW LEFT: Rush's striking genius captured in art.

modest and supremely hard-working – the embodiment of the Anfield team ethic that lay behind the club's domination of the game for almost 20 years. His singular talent, however, was a prized asset and so, when Juventus came calling in 1986, Rush made the move to Italy. It was not a happy spell. Rush famously could not settle, supposedly saying the experience was "like living in a foreign country". He went back to Liverpool and simply picked up where he left off.

By the time Rush finally did leave in 1996, Liverpool's all-conquering spell had been broken. He was transferred to Leeds United, before short stays at Sheffield United, Newcastle and Wrexham. Unsurprisingly, his extraordinary level of performance declined. Even for such a prodigious success as Rush there were disappointments, notably with a decent Welsh national side that missed out on qualifying for major championships. But the sheer bounty of goals and trophies at Liverpool, complemented by his all-round game, made Rush a legend for all the ages.

Soaring high
against QPR
in 1984.

"

*Painful to watch,
but beautiful.*

David Pleat after his side
conceded five to Rush

"

190

RIGHT: Arriving in Athens in 2007 to support the modern Liverpool in the Champions League final.

BELOW: Rush the goal machine.

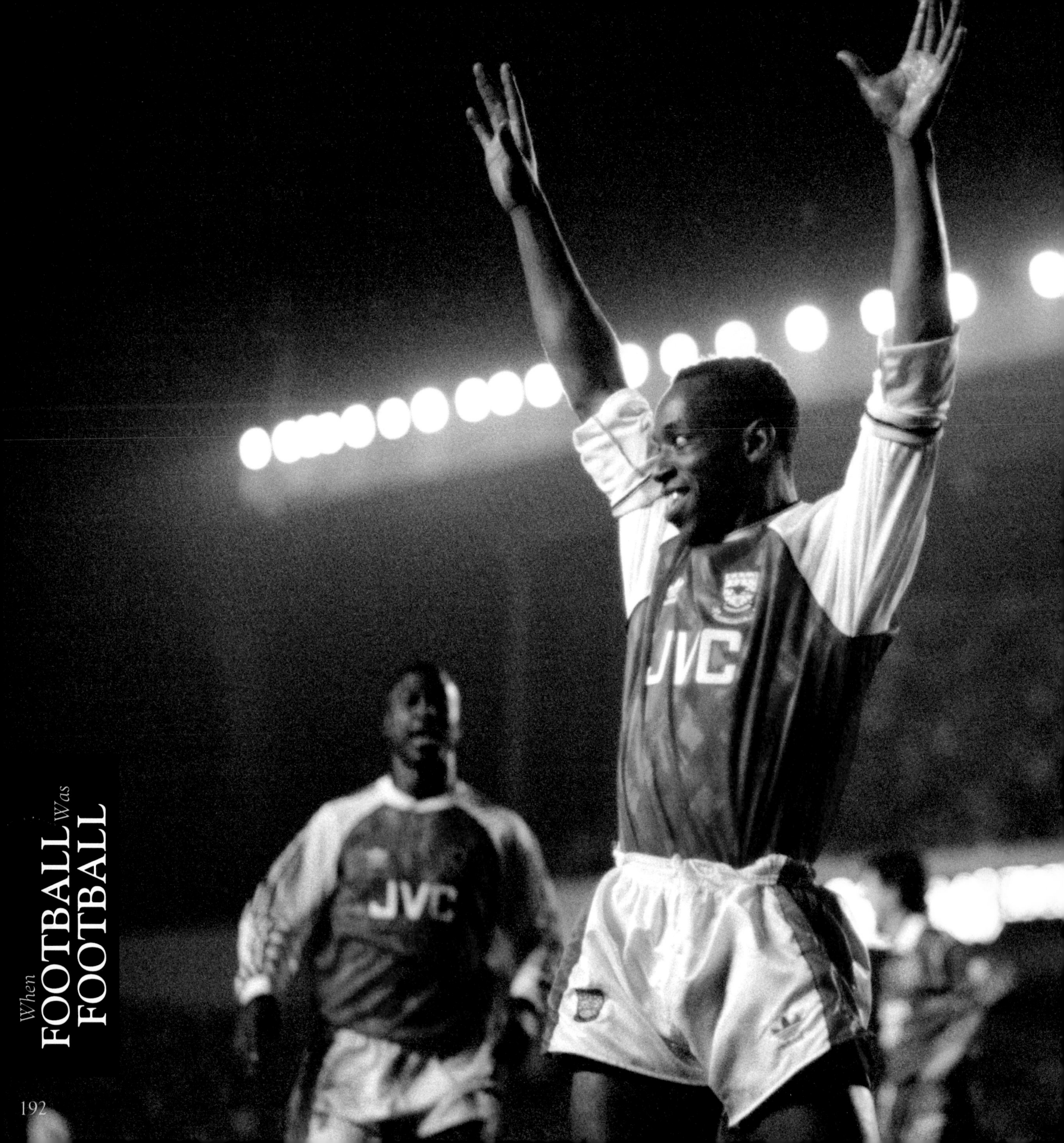
JVC
JVC

IAN WRIGHT

Wright came late to the professional game but made up for lost time with a record-breaking career at Arsenal and was a personality in tune with English football's confident revival.

> *"How can Arsenal be boring with players like Wright? I'd love him in my side.*
>
> Howard Kendall

Ian Wright celebrating his sixth goal in four games early on in his Arsenal career.

...vas all I ...for.

...ght

Ian Wright was one of those rare things: a partisan hero at one club who, now his playing days are over, is broadly popular among fans of many persuasions. Even Spurs supporters have a respect for the man identified as the ultimate modern Gooner legend.

His effervescent character was matched by his playing style. It often got him into confrontations and trouble, and he was never one to back down, particularly in the face of the lingering racism that still plagued the game. But his approach more often gained him goals, honours and adulation. Not a giant by any means, he was strong, quick and like a ball of lightning in and around the penalty area, scoring goals from all angles and tormenting defenders.

Wright's career and manner was a direct consequence of how he came into the pro ranks. He did not have the easiest starts, missing an absent father, enduring a difficult childhood and occasionally straying into trouble. Rejected as a youngster by League clubs, as he grew to adulthood he combined playing local football with work as a plasterer, until he spent a week in prison for non-payment of motoring fines. The experience shook Wright out of taking the wrong path in life, and his renewed persistence on the field was rewarded when he signed for Crystal Palace at the age of 21.

This was late by elite standards, but Wright set about exploiting the precious opportunity with zeal. He flourished at Selhurst Park, scoring in a losing FA Cup final and rejecting interest from Liverpool and Spurs, before joining Arsenal for a record fee in 1991. Wright and the Gunners were a perfect fit. His belligerent, confident style was ideally suited to manager George Graham's ethic, which was built on workrate, organization, a never-say-die attitude and a deliberately nurtured siege mentality. The goals and the trophies – both at home and abroad – soon flowed, culminating in Wright breaking Cliff Bastin's longstanding club record of 178 goals amid ecstatic scenes at Highbury.

For such a prolific, consistent striker, appearances for England were intermittent and somewhat bewilderingly few, but Wright was always committed and usually effective. He played his best football for England under manager Glenn Hoddle – whom he still calls "Gaffer" – but was robbed of the chance to play in the 1998 World Cup finals (and he had done a great deal to ensure England qualified for it) due to injury. Undaunted, he signed off from Arsenal with a Championship medal as Arsène Wenger set about transforming the club, before Wright became a popular player at West Ham, Nottingham Forest, Celtic and Burnley.

Retirement did not see Wright plump for management but instead a celebrity career. His personality was ideal for football's reinvigorated culture. As new fans were attracted to a sport largely free of its hooligan-blighted past, Wright was a compelling figure. The capacity crowds that now throng the Emirates were attracted not simply by Arsène Wenger's inspired success, but are a legacy of Wright's captivating way of playing and conducting himself off the pitch.

A music career may have been mercifully short lived, but television series and, more recently, high-profile punditry work, has shown Wright as well suited to the modern game in the satellite TV age. He began his career almost as a cliché – the parks footballer who made the most of his break to score at Wembley and win trophies – and is continuing today as an accomplished, confident communicator and a big-name former player who retains stellar appeal.

Club	Appearances	Goals
Crystal Palace	277	117
Arsenal	288	185
West Ham United	23	9
Nottingham Forest	10	5
Celtic	9	3
Burnley	15	4
Country	**Appearances**	**Goals**
England	33	9
TOTAL	**655**	**332**

Honours

League Title	1 (1997–98)
FA Cup	2 (1993, 1998)
League Cup	1 (1993)
European Cup Winners' Cup	1 (1994)

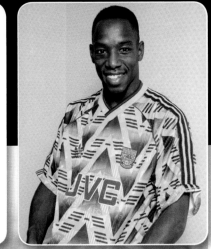

FOOTBALL
–STATS–

Ian Wright

Name: Ian Edward Wright

Born: Woolwich, London, 3rd November 1963

Position: Striker

Playing career: 1985–2000

RIGHT: Wright formed a great partnership and a close friendship with Mark Bright at Crystal Palace.

LEFT: Wright broke Cliff Bastin's Arsenal goalscoring record.

> My surname is always in the press. Some of the headlines write themselves.
>
> Ian Wright

In retirement, Wright has remained a prominent figure, comfortable in media work and as a host of his own TV shows. He has also put his celebrity to campaigning use, such as his involvement in 2007 with the Fit for Sport project to help children to participate in more sports.

One of the crowd: Gascoigne stands among the Newcastle faithful on the St James' Park terraces in September 1991.

PAUL GASCOIGNE

The most iconic footballer of the modern era, but also its most troubled, Paul Gascoigne was a world-class player whose talent was not fully realized, but he is a man who still enthrals.

When FOOTBALL Was FOOTBALL

During Tottenham's attempts to sign Paul Gascoigne in 1988, chairman Irving Scholar installed the player and assorted Geordie pals into a swish hotel just outside London. After a weekend of drunken mayhem, Scholar prepared to read Gascoigne the riot act. Instead, the youngster disarmed the Spurs supremo with the line "thank you for the best three days of our lives."

The story encapsulates much of what Paul Gascoigne has been about: by turns charming and maddening; captivating, charismatic, capable of great kindness and impossible not to like, but also infuriating, objectionable and hard to sympathize with. Reactions to Gascoigne are as complex and varied as the man himself. But everyone has an opinion on this most famous and controversial of all modern English footballers.

In assessing his eventful, often chaotic life, it is easy to forget just how great a player he was. He starred first for local side Newcastle, as a bona fide Geordie whom the fans on the Gallowgate End could readily identify with. Gascoigne played with a cheeky impetuosity, but also a potent vibrancy. Blessed with immaculate close control, he was already a brilliant reader of the game, scored goals and created hatfuls of chances. He was tireless, determined and brimmed with enthusiasm.

He was also a match-winner, and putting all those many qualities together made him the most coveted player in the game. Alex Ferguson and Manchester United were desperate to sign him, but it was Spurs, with new manager Terry Venables and Scholar spending money the club ultimately could not afford, who won Gascoigne's favour. He signed for a British record £2.2 million in July 1988.

Many warned that the bright lights of London would prove Gascoigne's undoing, but initially at least, he flourished. Gascoigne was the thrilling heartbeat of an inconsistent Spurs side. The team's form was unpredictable, but Gascoigne's reputation blossomed, leading to an England call-up. It was with the national team that he made his unforgettable impact on the wider game and beyond.

The star of the 1990 World Cup, his performances propelled England into their first semi-final for 24 years. There was the inevitable hard luck story as England crashed out on penalties, but Gascoigne's display, a mixture of brilliance and heartache following a booking that would have ruled him out of the final, was a pivotal episode in the history of the game. Gascoigne cried buckets of tears, the Gazza legend was born and football was never quite the same again.

The incredible reaction that Gascoigne and the England team received for their glorious failure rescued football from its deep decline and began its astonishing revival. Gascoigne was at the forefront – on talk shows, adverts and recording some truly dreadful pop songs. On the pitch where his talents

> *He's an intelligent boy who likes people to think he's stupid.*
>
> Ally McCoist

Gascoigne's finest hour, having just inspired Spurs to a famous 3-1 FA Cup semi-final victory over Arsenal in 1991.

Club	Appearances	Goals
Newcastle United	104	25
Tottenham Hotspur	110	33
Lazio	47	6
Rangers	108	38
Middlesbrough	48	4
Everton	38	1
Burnley	6	0
Boston United	5	0
Country	Appearances	Goals
England	57	10
TOTAL	**523**	**117**

Honours	
FA Cup	1 (1991)

FOOTBALL
–STATS–

Paul Gascoigne

Name: Paul John Gascoigne
Born: Gateshead, 27th May, 1967
Position: Midfielder
Playing career: 1985–2004

Performing 'Fog on the Tyne' with fellow Geordie legends, Lindisfarne.

really lay, it was a mixed picture. He almost single-handedly dragged Spurs to an FA Cup final in 1991, notably with one of the best goals ever seen at Wembley in an epic semi-final against Arsenal.

In would be the zenith of Gascoigne's career. He put himself out of the final after just a few minutes with a terrible challenge on Nottingham Forest's Gary Charles. It wrecked Gascoigne's knee, and though he was later presented with a winner's medal by his team-mates amid another flood of tears, it put in jeopardy a lucrative move to Italy – one that a bankruptcy-threatened Spurs were depending on.

Gascoigne did eventually make that move to Lazio, where he was hailed and analysed for his laddish character as much as his playing quality. He returned to Britain in 1995 and a lively spell at Rangers, before a succession of transfers to a variety of clubs, in search of that elusive form that had made him such a star in the first place. There were flashes of the old Gascoigne brilliance, particularly in an England shirt in the 1996 European Championships, but his best days were already behind him.

Dropped from the France '98 squad by manager Glenn Hoddle, Gascoigne flew into a violent rage. It was a clear signal of his fragile state of mind. Fame can be a damaging burden to carry and Gascoigne clearly suffered, veering from outlandish, often boorish escapades to debilitating introspection and chronic mental anguish. There were addictions – chiefly to booze – a chaotic and occasionally violent private life, public rows, assorted disgraces and reported suicide attempts, all played out in the glare of relentless publicity. Even now, a decade after he finally stopped playing, Gascoigne is still big box office and prime front-page material.

In his very public and ongoing struggles, Gascoigne has come to mirror George Best. He had the skill to match, too. While that wonderful genius never really realized its full potential, he remains the modern game's greatest and probably most flawed icon.

Tears of a clown: Gascoigne was consoled by England team-mate Terry Butcher after the unforgettable semi-final against West Germany in the 1990 World Cup in Turin.

Gazza had an infectious sense of humour but some refused to see the funny side. After referee Dougie Smith had dropped his yellow card during a match between Gascoigne's Rangers and Hibernian in December 1995, the England man jokingly cautioned Smith before handing him back his card. Smith promptly booked Gascoigne.

The incident during the 1991 FA Cup final that would plague Gascoigne for the rest
of his career. He lies in agony and with his knee cartilage in tatters, having just fouled
Nottingham Forest's Gary Charles (seen behind the referee).

Mobbed by Lazio team-mates after scoring a dramatic last-gasp
equalizer against local rivals Roma to secure a point in the Rome
derby, November 1992.

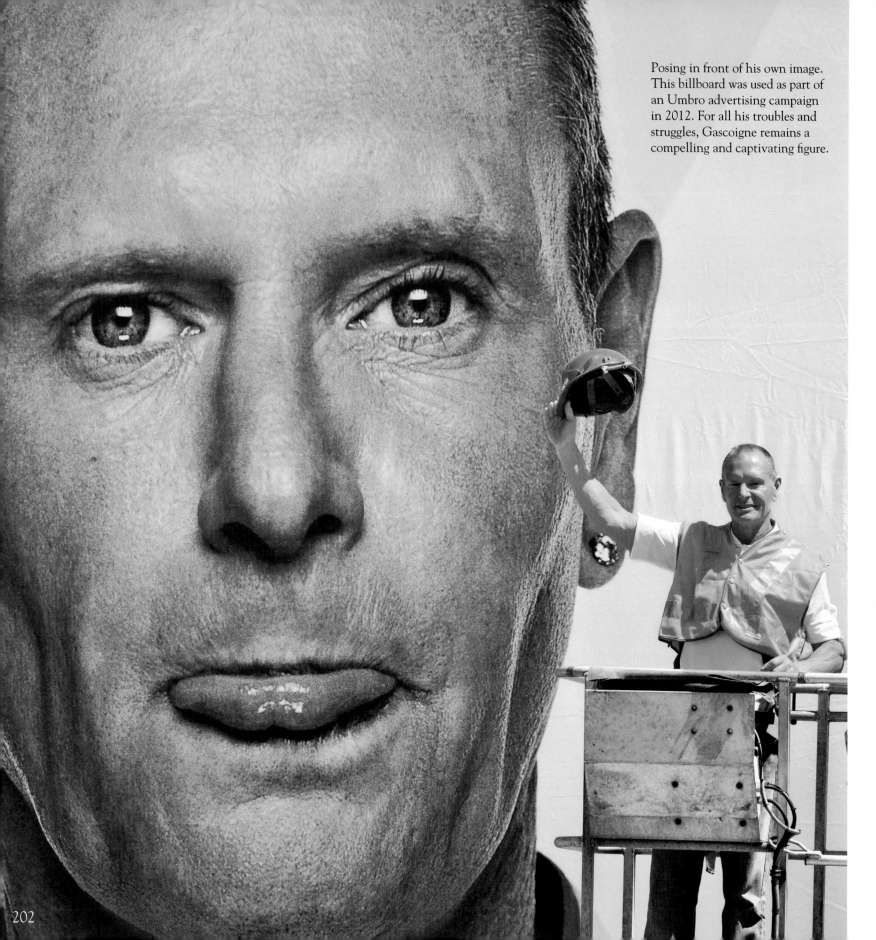

Posing in front of his own image. This billboard was used as part of an Umbro advertising campaign in 2012. For all his troubles and struggles, Gascoigne remains a compelling and captivating figure.

ALAN SHEARER

Alan Shearer is a modern great, a superstar of the Premier League era, but one who still represents traditional footballing virtues.

> " *I don't know what I'd have done if I hadn't become a footballer.* "
>
> Alan Shearer

A young Shearer in acrobatic action for Southampton in 1992.

Alan Shearer came to prominence over a half a century after Dixie Dean. While he was very much a footballer of the modern age, he shared some of the fundamental characteristics of Dean that made them such lethal strikers. Power, mental and physical toughness and technical skills in abundance marked each of them out – as of course did their goalscoring skills. The sport of football, particularly in terms of finance, may now be unrecognizable from its standing in the 1920s. But, for all that wealth, the most valuable currency of the multi-billion-pound industry in the new millennium has remained the same: goals.

Shearer scored bundles of them. He was a young footballer whose modest but effective consistency drew a host of admirers to covet his talent. He propelled one club towards an unlikely title triumph, became a folk hero in his hometown and ranks as one of England's greatest. Alan Shearer may not have as many medals to show off as some of his contemporaries, but few will be so cherished for so long, and by so many.

Hailing from the north-east production line that had given the game so many greats, it was surprising that he should not be signed by Newcastle but by a club at the other end of the country. At Southampton Shearer scored a hat-trick on his debut but thereafter made good, if not spectacular, progress. That improvement, however, and the level of performance in a side that was unlikely to challenge for honours, made him a transfer target. Most famously, Alex Ferguson and Manchester United wanted him. Instead, Shearer opted to join Jack Walker's Blackburn project for over £3.5 million – a huge fee for the time.

Shearer paid it back in spades. In tandem with Chris Sutton, Shearer led the "SAS" partnership that played such a big part in Rovers' League title win in 1994–95, his 34 League goals that season underpinning the achievement. It coincided with his elevation to world-class status and some great performances with the England team. Shearer had developed into one of the national side's most important players, and in the European Championships of 1996, he was top

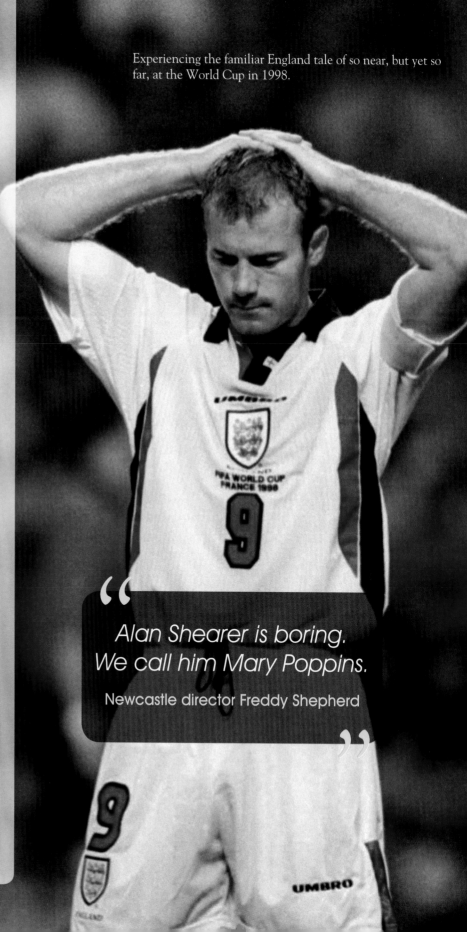

Experiencing the familiar England tale of so near, but yet so far, at the World Cup in 1998.

> "Alan Shearer is boring. We call him Mary Poppins."
>
> Newcastle director Freddy Shepherd

scorer as England agonizingly missed out on a dream win on home turf.

Once again Manchester United came calling, but while Shearer came close to a move to Old Trafford, he could not resist the lure of a return to his native Newcastle. Signed for a world record £15 million, Shearer was the key member of Kevin Keegan's continuing quest for an elusive title. That was not to happen. Managers came and went at St James' Park, but Shearer became a fixture, rattling in goals from all angles and distances. Injuries robbed him of much of his pace but he adapted his game to compensate, becoming more of a target man who could win the physical battle with defenders – something which did not quite endear him to opposition fans, but merely cemented his legendary status on Tyneside.

By the time of his retirement, Shearer had broken a host of club and League records and had slipped into a punditry role with the BBC rather than choosing to go into management. The call of his home club became too loud to ignore in 2009, however, and he returned to try to save Newcastle from relegation. It was not to be, but it certainly bolstered his idol status.

Shearer's career straddled two eras – before the Premier League and after it – that seem almost like different worlds, but in the adulation he received and the standing he has among fans – not only in Newcastle – he is that most traditional of football legends.

With *Match of the Day* partner, Gary Lineker. Shearer's critics label him as dull, but he has established himself as one of television's foremost pundits.

Club	Appearances	Goals
Southampton	158	43
Blackburn Rovers	172	131
Newcastle United	404	206

Country	Appearances	Goals
England	63	30
TOTAL	**797**	**410**

Honours

League Title   1 (1994–95)

FOOTBALL -STATS-

Alan Shearer

Name: Alan Shearer

Born: Gosforth, 13th August 1970

Position: Striker

Playing career: 1988–2006

Shearer (left) and his Blackburn strike partner Chris Sutton (right) were the joint recipients of the Carling Premier League Player of the Month trophy in November 1994, while manager Kenny Dalglish took the Manager of the Month award. It was a sign of Rovers' progress: the club would lift the League title that season.

" *It's an unbelievable
feeling for a Geordie,
scoring in front of
thousands of your
own people.*

Alan Shearer

"

Acknowledgements

Thanks to Dave Scripps, Simon Flavin and all at Mirrorpix, the team at Haynes, Paul Moreton, Kevin Gardner, Elizabeth Stone and Rebecca Ellis.

Very special thanks to Richard Havers.

And last – but definitely not least – the various *Mirror* journalists and photographers who told the story.

Select Bibliography

Charlton, Bobby, *Sir Bobby Charlton: My Manchester United Years* (Headline, 2007).
Cloake, Martin, *Danny Blanchflower* (ebook, Martin Cloake & Adam Powley, 2011).
Galvin, Robert, *The Football Hall of Fame* (Portico, 2011).
Henderson, John, *The Wizard* (Yellow Jersey, 2014).
Murphy, Pat, *His Way: Brian Clough* (Robson Books, 1994).
Rothmans Football Yearbook (various editions).
When Saturday Comes, *When Saturday Comes: The Half Decent Football Book* (Penguin, 2005).

Daily Mirror
Daily Telegraph
The Independent
The Guardian
The Times
Daily Mail
BBC
Englandfootballonline
Talksport